The Sales & Marketing MANAGEMENT
Guide to Sales Compensation Planning

COMMISSIONS BONUSES & BEYOND

William Keenan, Jr.

Editor

PROBUS
PUBLISHING

Chicago, Illinois
Cambridge, England

ISBN 1-55738-833-4

Printed in the United States of America

BB

1 2 3 4 5 6 7 8 9 0

CB

Table of Contents

About the Authors

Joanne M. Dahm is a sales compensation consultant for Hewitt Associates in Lincolnshire, Illinois. Assignments include incentive plan design, sales organization structures, and custom compensation surveys. She joined Hewitt Associates after a six-year career in sales, during which she managed major account relationships for a national producer of electronic publishing and imaging systems.

Frank X. Dowd is a principal in the Alexander & Alexander Consulting Group Compensation and Organizational Effectiveness practice, and is based in Greenwich, Connecticut. He is a past president of the Chicago chapter of the Society of Logistics Management and served on the White House Council for Productivity Improvement. He is a frequent speaker on variable compensation and is coeditor of the *Sales Compensation Handbook* (AMACOM, 1991).

Lisa Bush Hankin is a senior consultant with Sibson & Company, based in Baltimore, Maryland, for whom she's worked on a broad range of assignments, including organization effectiveness, executive compensation, and long-term incentive plan design. She's also written for the University of Michigan's *Human Resource Management Journal, Executive Excellence,* and *Management Focus.*

William Keenan, Jr. is the managing editor of *Sales & Marketing Management* magazine, and has written on sales, marketing, motivation, training, and compensation subjects for the past 15 years. He is the author of *Human Resources: A Planning Guide for Management* (Research Institute of America, 1984).

David C. Kuhlman is a principal in the Chicago office of Sibson & Company with a focus on sales compensation and long-term incentive plan design. Kuhlman is a member of the American Compensation Association and teaches the American Compensation Association course on sales compensation.

Maureen A. Meisner is a senior consultant with Sibson & Company in Chicago, with significant experience in sales force management and effectiveness. She is a member of the American Compensation Association and the Chicago Compensation Association.

Thomas R. Mott is the practice leader for sales compensation for Hewitt Associates in Lincolnshire, Illinois, typically focusing on incentive plan design and the integration of pay, performance, and company strategy. He speaks and writes frequently on sales compensation issues and is a member of the faculty for the American Compensation Association course on "The Compensation of Salespersons."

John K. Moynahan has been a management consultant for over 25 years, and retired as a vice-president of TPF&C (a Towers Perrin company). He now has an exclusive association with William M. Mercer, Incorporated. He has worked with clients on a wide range of sales and human resources issues and has designed sales incentive plans for over 150 companies. A frequent writer and lecturer on compensation issues, Moynahan is the author of *Designing an Effective Compensation Plan* (AMA-COM, 1980), *Incentive Compensation Workbook* (Bank Marketing Association, 1981), and *Sales Compensation Handbook* (AMA-COM, 1991).

William A. (Bill) O'Connell is a principal, Sibson & Company, Inc. Prior to joining Sibson he served as COO for GTN Industries and earlier headed the sales management practice at Personnel Corporation of America. In 1987 and 1989 he was the editor of the Dartnell *Survey of Sales Compensation.*

John F. Tallitsch is a principal and national practice leader for sales management and sales compensation consulting services for Buck Consultants, Inc., working out of the company's Cleveland office. He has 23 years of experience in compensation and sales management/compensation.

Craig Ulrich is a principal, leading William M. Mercer, Incorporated's Northeast Sales Compensation and Employee Performance Pay practices. Ulrich is a Certified Compensation Professional (CPC), a member of the American Compensation Association, and speaks and writes regularly on sales compensation and job evaluation/salary administration.

Preface

If it seems odd that a book on sales compensation concludes with a chapter presenting "the case against commissions," consider for a moment. The notion of the salesman-type—aggressive, entrepreneurial, self-starting, and driven by a pay system that's tied directly to performance—is something we've grown to take for granted. Even if a growing number of companies have decided that the type is not for them, they won't deny the type, its long history, or its record of success.

But times have changed, and the percentage of commission-only plans offered by American businesses has grown smaller. The very variety of sales compensation offerings, their complex combinations of base and incentive pay vehicles, the use of pay to drive new and difficult-to-measure sales behaviors, and the fact that so few companies will claim to have answered the sales compensation question satisfactorily—all suggest that there's still a lot of thinking to be done about how we pay salespeople.

Perhaps it's time to start thinking out of the box, as the creativity consultants would suggest—perhaps it's time to step outside of the set of established notions we have about pay, performance, and sales personalities, and how they interact.

Alfie Kohn's argument (presented in Chapter 12) is definitely out of the box. He argues that *all* reward systems are suspect and that *any* pay plan that ties pay to performance will only undermine the quality of performance over the long term. Read it. Few of us will agree with Kohn—particularly in all cases and for all companies—but all of us need to look a little more closely at what we're doing when we add an incentive "kicker" or a sales override, and all of us need to think harder about what we are likely to accomplish by such measures.

The truth is, if you look closely at the themes that run through all of the chapters of this collaboration, you'll find that the same concerns—quality, empowerment, teamwork, and customer focus—inform the work of all of the contributors.

"Sales compensation . . . is a communication tool with which an organization can articulate its goals internally, as well as to customers. . . . It can serve to align or manage the relationship between the customer's and the organization's interests," writes David Kuhlman in Chapter 1. "The drive toward total quality . . . has forced sales and marketing management to reassess not just the mix of behaviors required to perform the sales job, but also which behaviors lead to satisfied customers who continue to buy," says Craig Ulrich in Chapter 4. "When designed properly, team reward systems provide the necessary incentives to focus team members and the entire organization on those activities that are most valued by the customer," argues Maureen Meisner in Chapter 6.

My co-contributors also have a lot of practical advice to offer—from advice on implementing a new sales compensation plan (Chapter 8), to recommendations on using sales compensation as a recruitment and development tool (Chapter 9), to some caveats on sales *managers'* compensation.

There's even a look into the future of sales compensation—a future in which the quality movement continues to figure mightily. Bill O'Connell's and Lisa Bush Hankin's forward glance also includes a provacative prototype of sales compensation for the future—"life cycle sales compensation"— which might be well worth looking into right now.

In short, there's a lot going on, there's a lot to look forward to, and there's a lot to learn. Here's my hope that this collaboration helps move many readers along on that learning process.

Besides acknowledging the effort and work of the by-lined contributors to this collection, I'd like to thank Francesca Morton, for her help in preparing the manuscripts, and Tony Rutigliano, publisher of *Sales & Marketing Management* magazine, for his unstinting support of the entire project.

Introduction

Beyond the Basics

By William Keenan, Jr., Managing Editor
Sales & Marketing Management magazine

Bring any group of salespeople together to tell them that you're going to be changing their compensation plan, and you'll hear an uproar. That's in part because they think they're going to be shortchanged—that the adjustments or modifications that you're introducing are going to cheat them out of commissions, manipulate them to produce more for the same amount of pay, or award someone else a bonus that should be going to them.

I've seen salespeople threaten to quit over changes—even minor changes—in their compensation plans, and I've seen companies go to extremes to try to take the minds of salespeople off the changes.

In one case, for instance, the vice-president of sales for a multimedia communications company hired a professional wrestler to pose as a salesperson at the company's annual sales meeting. When the sales VP announced the change in the compensation plan and started to go through the details, the wrestler-cum-salesperson charged the front of the room, lifted the sales VP off

There's no plan—no matter how well it fits your company's needs today— that will continue to be perfect. □

the ground, held him over his head, and threatened to toss him to the back of the room if he didn't leave the compensation plan well enough alone. At this point the company's regional sales managers rushed up to the front of the room to calm the "angry" salesperson by explaining the virtues of the new plan and showing how a salesperson—by maintaining this level of performance here and making a few more of that type of sale there— could make even more money under the new pay arrangement.

The beast was appeased, the hoax was revealed, and the audience of salespeople applauded what was, in effect, the sales executive's effort to preempt what he thought would be their own inevitable reaction. It worked. He was able to put off a lot of questions and angry debate, but he wasn't able to eliminate the grumbling.

It's an extreme example of how to implement a new sales compensation plan, undoubtedly—but not unbelievable. In a recent discussion group conducted by *Sales & Marketing Management* on the issue of sales compensation, four of the six sales professionals participating said they had made their last job change as a result of a compensation dispute. All argued that "arbitrary" changes in their respective companies' compensation practice or policy had cheated them out of commissions or bonuses that they felt they were entitled to.

The other two people in the group were sales managers.

You can't expect salespeople to adopt new behaviors if they're being rewarded for something else. □

That's the context in which any changes in your company's compensation plan are going to take place. And as you must realize, change is inevitable. There's no one-size-fits-all plan, and there's no plan—no matter how well it fits your company's needs today—that will continue to be perfect as your company's business grows, as the marketplace changes, and as sales strategies are adjusted to meet the needs of evolving customer demands.

Customer satisfaction levels, team selling, diversified sales roles, postsale relationships, quality management, alternative sales channels, and other new and evolving elements in business relationships will all have an impact on your company's compensation plan for one compelling reason—you can't expect salespeople to adopt new behaviors if they're being rewarded for something else—i.e., you can't expect them to build long-term relationships with target customers if you're paying them on the basis of how much they get out the door this month.

Sales compensation cannot lead a company's strategy—you can't just add a customer satisfaction bonus and sit back to wait for customer satisfaction levels to increase—but you can work your compensation plan effectively to reinforce your company's business plan.

You'll be able to explain the reasons and the goals of your plan succinctly enough, and convincingly enough, that you won't have to worry about getting tossed on your ear. □

The truth is, you *will* be changing your company's compensation plan—if not today, then in a few months, certainly within the next year or two. What we hope to offer in the pages that follow are some of the reasons, tactics, and strategies from top compensation specialists who have already covered some of the ground in the direction that you're headed. I think that they have enough to offer so that you'll be able to traverse some of that ground effectively yourself—and explain the reasons and the goals of your evolving sales compensation plan succinctly enough, and convincingly enough, that you won't have to worry about getting tossed on your ear.

Chapter 1

Implementing Business Strategy through Sales Compensation

By David C. Kuhlman, Principal
Sibson & Company

Introduction

As a start-up company, a high-tech firm had taken the market by storm with a first-rate product in a developing market and had built its success by paying its sales force to develop new accounts. Just ten years later, though, the company was struggling to remain profitable. The problem was that, as its overall business strategy changed to meet new marketplace challenges, the company failed to make corresponding sales compensation changes. In fact, the company made several fundamental—and critical— sales compensation errors. First, salespeople were not being paid to penetrate existing accounts, only to develop new ones. As a result, not only did the potential for account penetration among

The company's sales compensation plan was not only misaligned with the changing business strategy, but it was undermining the achievement of that strategy. ☐

the existing customer base remain unassessed, but the needs of those customers were not being met—leaving them vulnerable to defection to competitors. In addition, the pay plan also discouraged team selling—another strategy necessary for the company to meet its customers' needs and increase profitability. Because the pay plan provided the greatest personal reward for finding new customers and making new sales, that is exactly what the sales force did. The company's sales compensation plan was not only misaligned with the changing business strategy, but it was undermining the achievement of that strategy. Sales compensation had become a significant barrier to a steady and growing level of profitability.

For many companies, this is an all-too-familiar story. Many of today's largest sales forces are undergoing major organization change and renewal efforts to keep pace with increasing customer and competitive expectations. Successful companies are constantly on the lookout for opportunities to better meet customer needs. And almost without exception, these efforts include a reconfiguration or, increasingly, a complete redesign of the sales compensation system to keep it aligned with changes to the overall strategy of the business.

When making such changes to the organization, companies must ensure that sales compensation remains closely linked to overall business strategy and goals—a critical factor in the success of any enterprise. Misalignment between business strategy and sales compensation will, at a minimum, inhibit performance and can, in extreme cases, endanger the company's success. There are many situations, similar to that of the high-tech company described above, in which a dysfunctional sales compensation system hobbled an otherwise healthy business.

Sales compensation is a communication tool with which an organization can articulate its goals. □

Sales compensation is much more than a way to determine rewards for salespeople. Sales compensation is a communication tool with which an organization can articulate its goals internally, as well as to its customers and the rest of the outside world. It can also serve to align or manage the relationship between the customer's and the organization's interests. And it can help reduce the inevitable internal conflicts that arise in every organization over pricing, market segmentation, product line emphasis, and after-sale service.

How, then, can a company put the power of sales compensation to work to achieve its articulated business strategy and organizational goals?

Finding the Right Role for Pay

Sales compensation can help reinforce change and solve problems. □

A properly planned, designed, and implemented sales compensation system is a powerful instrument for implementing and reinforcing business strategy. At the same time, however, it is not a panacea, and its range of effectiveness is somewhat more limited than most sales managers like to believe. Sales compensation can help reinforce change and solve problems. It can also increase sales to new customers, increase profitability, reforge the link between sales and service, improve accounts receivable, get the engineering staff involved in the sales process, and accomplish a host of other goals.

But a single plan can't accomplish all these goals at once. And companies can't expect a sales compensation program alone to accomplish their business objectives or to blaze the trail of change. Rather than being a leading lever of change, sales compensation can serve as a confirming anchor of a new way of thinking.

By nature, sales compensation should lead change somewhat because salespeople are inherently more money-motivated than other employees in the organization and tend to look to the pay plan for signals of the right kinds of behaviors. But companies must take care that sales compensation does not get too far ahead of the rest of the organization. As one sales executive put it, "Leadership is being out in front, leading the troops—but not being so far out that they mistake you for the enemy and shoot you instead." In short, pushing too much change through sales compensation can lead to a collapse in confidence in the plan and a breakdown in performance in the field.

If a company ignores these fundamental tenets when designing a sales compensation program, the end result is usually a plan that confuses the sales force by sending too many, often conflicting, signals about what is important to the success of the company and also is too difficult to understand. And the more complex the plan is, the higher its risk of collapse. (See Exhibit 1.1.) A good rule of thumb here is that a sales compensation plan is too com-

"Leadership is being out in front, leading the troops—
but not being so far out that they mistake you for the enemy and shoot you instead." □

plex if (1) it can't be explained in the time it takes the elevator to get from the tenth floor of the building to the lobby (the "Elevator Rule") or (2) its calculations can't be completely worked out on the back of a business-size envelope (the "Envelope Rule").

When a large health-care company wanted its salespeople to make a transition quickly from managing customer transactions to managing territories as profitable "fran-

Exhibit 1.1

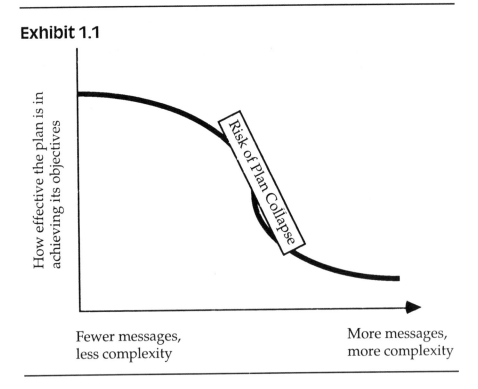

How effective the plan is in achieving its objectives

Fewer messages, less complexity

More messages, more complexity

chises," it did so through a new compensation plan that introduced a powerful pay-for-profit component. At first, the sales force embraced the new concept. But, since there were numerous aspects of the overall selling process that forced salespeople to use their old ways of selling, they were not effective at managing for profits, and they experienced pay declines. Eventually, through a great expenditure of internal resources, the sales force succeeded in getting the company to retract the new "profit" plan and reinstate a version of the old pay plan. In retrospect, virtually all those involved, including those who rejected the plan, agree that "it was basically the right thing for the business." The problems stemmed from pushing through too much change too fast. If the changes the plan contemplated had been implemented over the course of several years, it likely would have worked. But as it turned out, the combination of a significant increase in plan complexity with significantly changed measures overloaded the plan and caused it to collapse.

One way to send performance signals without overburdening the core compensation plan is through sales contests and recognition programs. □

One way to send performance signals without overburdening the core compensation plan is through sales contests and recognition programs. It is easy to overlook the impact of such "corny" things as

Recognition and contests must be woven into an overall reward strategy that supports the organization's business and sales strategies. □

the recognition dinner at the national sales meeting or the President's Club ring. But this type of recognition works if it:

■ Is distinguished from the core compensation program through different measures or standards of performance

■ Does not limit winners to a fixed number; is promoted throughout the year via updates, rankings, and the like

■ Does not overwhelm the core compensation plan with a large or overly prominent contest that creates a distinctly different "winners list" and "earners list"

The important thing to remember is that recognition and contests must be woven into an overall reward strategy that supports the organization's business and sales strategies.

The Strategy-Compensation Link

Clearly, sales compensation is an important tool for implementing organizational and sales strategy. Sales forces today face a bewildering muddle of business imperatives and technique-of-the-moment buzzwords that offer the promise of radically improved performance. At the same time, sales forces must still answer some basic questions about how they will operate:

1. Will teams be rewarded? And, if so, how?

2. Will profit, profitability, or growth be rewarded?

3. Should the customer service function be eligible for incentives?

4. How will the new reengineered pricing process affect sales compensation?

Not surprisingly, organizations have difficulty untangling business imperatives from nice-to-have elements of sales compensation. So the key to fulfilling an organization's business needs without an overly complex compensation plan is to tie each aspect of compensation back to the organization's business and sales strategies. These tie-ins to business and sales strategy concentrate on a set of needs that cascade down from the most strategic— "What attractive and profitable new markets do we want to penetrate?"—to the most tactical and prosaic—"What can the information system track?" A framework for thinking about this cascade is illustrated in Exhibit 1.2.

Organizations have difficulty untangling business imperatives from nice-to-have elements of sales compensation. ☐

Exhibit 1.2

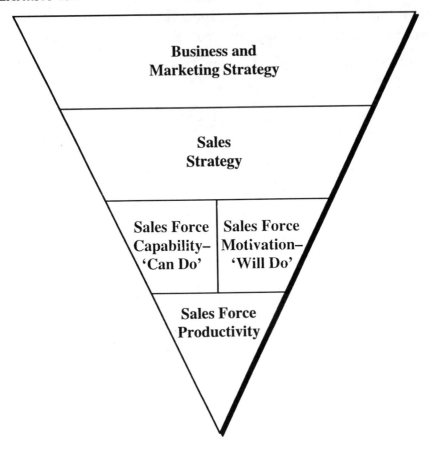

The Business Strategy

The company must first articulate its business and marketing strategies to establish the overall goals of the sales and service organization and, by extension, the goals of the compensation program. Business strategy defines success for the sales compensation program and provides some of the first-order boundaries of the program—i.e., what the program will *not* do. Exhibit 1.3 provides other examples of how the business and marketing strategies affect sales compensation. The key questions to ask about strategy are:

Using its sales strategy, a company must next articulate clearly how it will approach the market with its products and its offering. □

1. What does our strategy require that we accomplish with our customers?

2. How will that accomplishment be measured or show itself tangibly?

3. What traditional markets, products, customer segments, or sales approaches are omitted?

4. What constraints are we operating under?

The Sales Strategy

Using its sales strategy, a company must next articulate clearly how it will approach the market with its products and its offering—that is, specific customer adaptations, delivery, post-sale service, and the like. For example, by providing exceptional post-sales service for many years,

Exhibit 1.3

Element of Business and Marketing Strategy	What It Defines or Dictates	Examples of How Sales Compensation Should Adapt
Product definition	• What is the relative competitiveness of the intrinsic features of the product? • What nonproduct value-added does the company offer? • What is the projected life cycle and possible obsolescence of the product?	• How prominent, aggressive, or active should sales reps be? • Who should be included on the selling team? • What should sales reps be rewarded for selling (e.g., products, services, integrated systems)? • How should the sales compensation plan contribute to product successorship? How will a managed transition be achieved?
Target markets	• Relative attractiveness of types of customers • Channels of distribution • Geographic focus and objectives • Emphasis on penetration of current customers versus acquisition of "new names"	• How will the program address cross-channel sales credit issues? Will, for example, every sales rep be credited for every dollar of sales within their geographic area regardless of their direct involvement? • Will we encourage a focus on certain customers or segments? • How will such things as performance standards and target markets reflect geographic differences? • Will we encourage "missionary selling" or selling to current customers? • Are we encouraging the right behaviors (e.g., follow-up) to get the kind of penetration we want?
Financial plans	• Revenue and profit targets • Capacity or break-even levels	• What will performance measures emphasize: revenues or profits? • Is profitability (in terms of margin) or sales profit contribution an issue? • How much "stretch" is built into plans and therefore how much aggressiveness is needed in the field? • How will payout formulas recognize business-based financial hurdles or capacity constraints?

IBM's sales force was able to sustain the company despite its "fast-follower" technology strategy. In an environment that emphasizes post-sale service, it is the persistence and penetration of customer accounts and the overall profitability of providing service (whether sold or not) that drive sales compensation.

The company's selling approach also has a profound effect on sales compensation, as movement up or down the selling pyramid affects the suitability of old reward systems or the need to redesign them. (See Exhibit 1.4.) For example, a number of major database software developers are discovering that market forces have invalidated their traditional selling approach. The commoditization of core products, the appearance and prominence of niche players, and more rapid technological obsolescence have sent these companies scrambling to change their sales approach from feature and relationship selling to a needs and partnership selling approach. These companies have responded to this changing marketplace by developing industry specialist sales forces, more customer-prominent technical salespeople, and new "consulting" organizations selling fee-for-service adaptation of the product.

Major database software developers are discovering that market forces have invalidated their traditional selling approach. □

Exhibit 1.4   Sales Strategy at a Glance: The Selling Pyramid

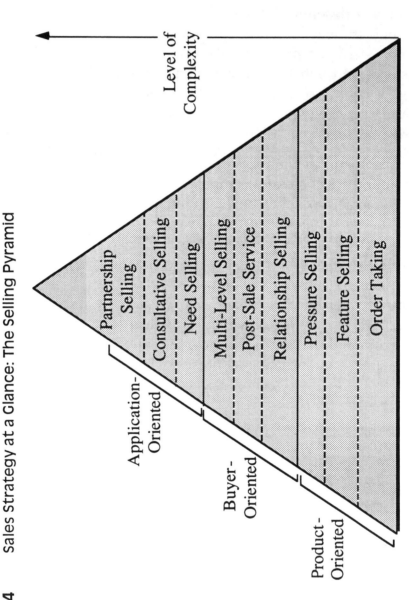

At the same time, these companies are also creating a potential sales compensation disaster. For example, some companies have changed traditional commission schemes to include double counting sales by industry specialists, goals that increase 30 percent to 70 percent per year to accommodate supposedly enhanced productivity and cost, and commission rates that have been "adjusted" to balance product and service sales. And the end result has been frustration and turnover in sales staffs, missed opportunities, and confusion in the customer base, including among "tried and true" customers.

Where the sales strategy is significantly different from that of competitors, potential pay competitiveness and turnover problems must be factored into compensation plan designs. □

As this example so clearly illustrates, sales strategy affects compensation plans profoundly. Exhibit 1.5 illustrates some of the key compensation considerations for major sales strategies.

Sales strategy has two other dimensions that play into sales compensation. First, where the sales strategy is significantly different from that of competitors, potential pay competitiveness and turnover problems must be factored into compensation plan designs. In addition, compensation plans must recognize the effort and motivation required to change the way an industry values providers' selling efforts.

Secondly, some organizations follow industry-standard sales approaches but attempt to out-execute their competitors. In these situations, compensation plans must be carefully crafted to send the right signals about timeliness, service, and how the sales force will differentiate itself. Except

Exhibit 1.5

Selling Strategy		Frequent Compensation Questions
Application-oriented strategies	Partnership selling Consultative selling Needs selling	• How will other members of the "team" be integrated? • How will capacity-filling, fixed-cost-covering tangible products be balanced with lucrative services? • How will we assess customer satisfaction and impact on their operation?
Buyer-oriented strategies	Multilevel selling Postsale service Relationship selling	• How will longer selling cycles and penetration selling be factored in? • How will we encourage truly (and mutually) profitable commitments to service and support? • How will we recognize annuity sales and reward true differential value-added by the individual?
Product-oriented strategies	Pressure selling Feature selling Order taking	• How can we balance the need for aggressiveness and any sort of management control? • Will we reward product mix in any way? • Will compensation plans recognize territory potential or just actual dollars delivered?

for sales approaches very "low" on the pyramid, compensation plans designed to encourage "better execution" often backfire by encouraging aggressiveness in situations that really require attentiveness.

Sales Force "Can Do" versus "Will Do"

Even when guided by clear strategic goals and bounded by an effective sales strategy, sales compensation plans must get past gritty tactical obstacles. "Nobody likes to sell the new product because it is on allocation." "Measuring return on investment at the account level is all well and good, but nobody can agree on how to allocate costs." Such comments from salespeople are typical when a new pay program is introduced. The fact is, no matter how well designed the pay plan is and how closely it is linked to the business strategy, it will not succeed unless the sales force can and will make it succeed. These basic tactical concerns involve the real ground-level considerations to which all sales compensation plans must respond—or fail.

For example, if its sales force serves multiple lines of business, multiple manufactur-

No matter how well designed the pay plan is and how closely it is linked to the business strategy, it will not succeed unless the sales force can and will make it succeed. □

Systems constraints are the most frequent can-do obstacle to implementing an effective compensation program. □

ing options, and different product lines, a company should design a sales compensation plan that recognizes differences among products or lines of business. In doing so, the company will help counteract natural momentum in product mix toward those products that yield a larger transaction, require less effort, have shorter selling cycles, have a more familiar customer base, or lend themselves to tried-and-true selling processes.

These considerations fall into two categories: capabilities—sales force "Can Do," and the motivational—sales force "Will Do"(see Exhibit 1.6).

"Can Do"

Two frequent can-do issues are systems constraints and sales management capability.

Systems constraints are the most frequent can-do obstacle to implementing an effective compensation program. Efforts to reward profitability often run aground on an inability to measure profit on an account level, the absence of an accurate and defensible cost allocation methodology, and an unwillingness to share gross margin information in the field. In addition, the information required to communicate performance levels to the field between paychecks frequently requires a level of detail and sophistication that many transaction-oriented systems lack.

And the unavoidable truth is that many systems issues are difficult to resolve without significant investment. This is especially true in environments with a high transaction volume or where product lines or customer relationships are complex. Still, there are some things that can be done to address these issues:

1. Run manual systems if transaction volume is low or "fragmentary" reports are available.

The unavoidable truth is that many systems issues are difficult to resolve without significant investment. □

Exhibit 1.6

"Can Do" Issues	"Will Do" Issues
• Structural constraints or capabilities such as service organizations or geographic coverage	• Aggressiveness in the field
• Systems constraints	• Willingness/capability to sell more difficult products and customers
• Quality and orientation of sales management	• Track record in achieving more qualitative, "managed" results
• Product characteristics and manufacturing capabilities	• Cooperative or collaborative culture within the sales force and cross-functionally
• Job design/decision rights	• Performance measurement
• Skills and abilities	

Sales compensation programs, no matter how sophisticated, clear, or motivational, cannot overcome significant field management weakness. □

2. If reports of the elements of bottom-line results—sales volume, margin, accounts receivable, inventory costs, and so on—are often unreliable, publish these reports by rep throughout the region and let peer pressure do the rest.

3. If a clean regional bottom-line number is available, consider paying all reps in the region on those bottom-line results.

4. Cost allocations, particularly overhead allocation, are frequently—but not always—red herrings. If overhead allocation rates are consistent and built into budgeted cost, it makes little difference how the sale is made. Indeed, where product manufacturing costs are allocated, precise cost accounting is needed only where reps can influence manufactured cost. And where costs are included as a benchmark for managing pricing, standard unit cost allocation is frequently good enough.

For their part, first-line sales management can make or break a new compensation program. The more significant the change in behavior required in the field, the more important sales management becomes. Sales compensation programs, no matter how sophisticated, clear, or motivational, cannot overcome significant field management weakness. And the stronger field management is, the more sophisticated compensation program a field organization can sustain.

A good litmus test to assess the sophistication of first-line sales managers follows. "Yes" answers to these questions indicate a fairly high level of sophistication among sales management, so the company can plan on developing a fairly sophisticated pay plan. On the other hand, "no" answers indicate that sales management may need significant development to undertake a more sophisticated sales management approach. Make no mistake: sales compensation success or failure as often stems from management execution as from any strength or weakness in the plan itself.

Sales compensation success or failure as often stems from management execution as from any strength or weakness in the plan itself. □

- Do you provide complete, "business-level" performance reporting to sales managers?

- Have you been doing so for more than 18 months?

- Do first-level sales managers demonstrate a command of the facts in their performance reports when questioned?

- Do the business plans developed and submitted by first-level sales managers indicate a level of sophistication and understanding of the full range of the company's activities?

■ Does your sales management corps contain a healthy percentage, say 20 percent to 30 percent, of individuals who came from outside the sales force?

A classic will-do issue is the willingness of a sales force to take on a new product. □

■ Do you have a history of rotating first-line sales managers in and out of staff positions or up into senior management?

■ Do finance, manufacturing, and marketing work well with first-line sales managers and interact with them frequently?

■ Does the incentive program encompass the true economics of the operation for first-level sales managers?

"Will Do"

A classic will-do issue is the willingness of a sales force to take on a new product. When the sales organization adds a new or distinct product, it should provide additional emphasis on that product in the pay plan. But this emphasis should not be limited to simply rewarding product profitability while ignoring such things as factory capacity or selling lead time. For example, if selling lead time is not recognized in the pay plan, the sales force will concentrate on big-ticket, big-profit items that require six to twelve months to close, as well as smaller units that are easier and faster sales. In this environment, organizations attempting product successorship—say, from a traditional mechanical product to its '90s electronic version—may see the volume of the traditional product plummet far more quickly than they anticipated while new product sales increase exactly as planned—that is, slowly. Avoiding this sort of trap involves balancing not only the desired product mix, but the potential market demand. If the sales force is to resist a market trend, salespeople usually have to be paid handsomely for their efforts. Another approach emphasizes balance by conditioning rewards for one product on the quota fulfillment for another. However, interlocking performance measures that require salespeople to hit quota on both to earn a payout backfire at least as often as they succeed.

If the sales force is to resist a market trend, salespeople usually have to be paid handsomely for their efforts. □

Many organizations design a sales compensation program that recognizes these organizational pluses and minuses and adapts accordingly only after the change effort has run aground. These plans not only lead the main direction of sales organization change, but help work around or fix such limitations as sales management or systems that are not quite up to the task, building lines of communication, and the like. It is when sales compensation does not adapt to these realities that these plans disconnect from the organization's strategy—and the problems begin.

A Tool for Change: Handle with Care

It is a mistake to downplay or forget the importance and significance that salespeople attach to the pay program. □

As all this indicates, there is much more to linking sales compensation to strategy than meets the eye. Yet, it is a mistake to downplay or forget the importance and significance that salespeople attach to the pay program. If not designed with care, a pay plan will not only undermine the company's business strategy, but it could also instigate unwanted turnover or, worse, a sales volume shortfall.

Given the dysfunctional nature of a poorly designed sales compensation plan with a tenuous link to overall strategy, it is imperative that companies approach the design of these plans from the right direction. Make no mistake, the right compensation plan can help the strategy gain a secure foothold in the organization by motivating and rewarding the types of behaviors that will improve share, volume, and profitability. But the company must take care when developing that plan.

Companies that pay careful attention to how they sell are able to integrate their sales forces into the fabric of their business and marketing strategies. In a competitive environment in which the customer reigns, the essential elements of choosing the right compensation plan must not be forgotten.

Chapter 2

The Five Most Popular Sales Compensation Plans

By John K. Moynahan, Consultant
William M. Mercer, Incorporated

Introduction

While each sales compensation program has to be developed to match the specifics of an organization's strategy, values, and customer/market interface, there are nonetheless five generic formats into which virtually all contemporary sales compensation programs fit:

1. Base Salary

2. Straight Commission

3. Combination Plans: Salary/Commission (low-risk)

4. Combination Plans: Salary/Commission (high-risk)

5. Combination Plans: Salary/Bonus

To understand sales compensation, one needs to be familiar with two concepts that dictate, almost completely, the level and variability of sales compensation: Prominence in the Marketing Mix and Barrier to Entry.

The higher the prominence in the marketing mix, the greater the opportunity to create added value through creative salesmanship. ☐

Prominence in the Marketing Mix is an indicator of the relative importance of field sales in comparison with all other factors influencing the buying decision. If, for example, the combined effects of a company's advertising, promotions, and pricing are primarily responsible for its success, then the field sales rep is low in prominence; at the other extreme, if the sales rep must personally find and qualify prospects, and then through creative "salesmanship" entice the buyer toward the employer's product, process, or service, then the sales rep has high prominence in the marketing mix.

While most sales positions fall between the extremes of prominence (or vary by customer segment—for example, high for new accounts but low for repeat customers), the general relationship between prominence and pay is intuitively apparent; the higher the prominence in the marketing mix, the greater the opportunity to create added value through creative salesmanship and, therefore, the greater the emphasis on variable pay (commission or bonus) in the compensation package.

Barrier to Entry is an indication of the scarcity of individuals with the educational and/or experiential credentials sufficient to meet the minimum job requirements. Barrier to entry, therefore, influences the level of secure compensation in the compensation package. If the nature of the sales role is such that an advanced degree and/or years of experience is needed simply to fulfill the basic job requirements, then one would expect to find a higher level of secure compensation (usually base salary) in the compensation package than where the available labor pool satisfying minimal job requirements is large.

If an advanced degree and/or years of experience is needed simply to fulfill the basic job requirements, then one would expect to find a higher level of secure compensation in the compensation package. □

The notion of *risk* in the compensation package also needs to be understood. Compensation that is "at risk" is any compensation opportunity that the recipient might receive none of. "Low-risk" compensation is a portion of earnings (such as salary) that the recipient is virtually assured of receiving regardless of productivity. Thus, it is overly simplistic to consider all incentives, even commissions, to be "at risk"; one needs to examine the program further to determine the minimum amount

The higher the prominence of the field sales role in the marketing mix, the riskier should be the program. ☐

of incentive or bonus the least productive plan participant could receive and consider only the remaining earnings to be truly "at risk." Base salary is generally (but not always) low-risk compensation, but frequently much of the variable or "incentive" component of the package is low-risk as well (or as assured as salary, e.g., first dollar commission is a situation in which zero sales is impossible). Thus, examining the nominal proportions (e.g., 80 percent salary, 20 percent incentive, or a "50/50" plan, salary and commission) provides no insight into the true risk inherent in the package.

It is clear that, in general, the higher the prominence of the field sales role in the marketing mix, the riskier should be the program. And, indeed, that concept is reflected in the design of contemporary sales compensation systems.

Simply put, a sales compensation program should be a "win-win" economic game, where the recipient receives a combination of low-risk and high-risk compensation appropriate to the prominence and barrier of the job. Base salary reflects the barrier to entry of the position, and incentive pay (bonus and commission) contains a level of true risk appropriate to the prominence of the sales position. The overwhelming majority of contemporary compensation plans are "packaged" as Base Salary, Straight Commission, or Combination (Salary plus Incentive) programs. The Combination category needs to be segmented further, for under this same heading are found plans that are dramatically different from each other in terms of risk; thus the Salary plus Incentive category will be represented by three compensation designs: Salary plus Incentive (Low-Risk), Salary plus Incentive (High-Risk), and Salary plus Bonus.

In the remainder of this chapter, each of these five approaches is defined and illustrated. Additionally, some general guidance is offered concerning the implications, advantages, and disadvantages of each of the five general models.

The majority of contemporary compensation plans are "packaged" as Base Salary, Straight Commission, or Combination (Salary plus Incentive) programs. □

Base Salary

Base salary can be defined as a fixed sum of money paid at regular intervals, usually every two weeks or twice a month. Base salaries are normally established based on experience, seniority, merit, or other characteristics of the incumbent. Positions, including sales jobs, are slotted into an overall compensation hierarchy administered for all salaried employees, and reviewed annually according to performance.

Base salary is the exclusive source of compensation for the vast majority of American employees. □

Base salary is an entirely familiar concept to most business people, regardless of function. In fact (with the exception of sales functions), base salary is the exclusive source of compensation for the vast majority of American employees.

Salary-only plans have a variety of advantages:

■ Provides a stable, predictable income stream.

■ Allows management to stress training and team sales, as well as support and servicing activities of sales reps, without "hurting" the individual's earnings.

■ Minimizes sales administration requirements (quota-setting, commission calculations, etc.); easy to communicate and understand.

■ Facilitates switching or realigning territories.

■ Fixes a large component of sales expense.

■ Treats sales reps comparably to "peers" in nonsales functions.

But, in some situations, companies have found significant problems with salary-only plans. For instance, they:

■ May require more management "motivation" of sales force, since there is no monetary incentive to reinforce management's directives.

■ Do not directly reward extra effort in the short term.

■ Place a high degree of emphasis on merit pay and performance appraisal programs to recognize exceptional contributors. Sufficient flexibility is often lacking.

■ Require highly skilled management, since there are no financial incentives to reinforce the company's sales objectives.

■ Can make it difficult to retain the most talented sales reps if competitors offer variable incentive compensation. May result in retention of mediocre performers.

"Base salary only" compensation programs for sales representatives are appropriate where:

Companies have found significant problems with salary-only plans. □

The sales role is either highly consultative or highly service oriented. □

1. The industry is mature and stable with established buying practices, long sales cycles, and multiyear contracts for services.

2. The company's market position is secure, with an established base of repeat customers.

3. The sales role is either highly consultative or highly service oriented. Consultative sales frequently involve substantial investigation of needs, identification of solutions, and persuasive advising over a period of weeks or years. Service sales usually require significant pre- and postsale follow-through by the salesperson with other internal functions.

4. The sales process is either lengthy, team-oriented, or service-oriented; frequently, it is difficult to measure individual performance.

5. The "barrier to entry" is high. In consultative sales positions, the technical skills needed are often substantial; this is usually reflected in high base salaries (and frequently, a "salary-only" program).

Straight Commission

A commission can be defined as "equity in a business result"; the sales rep shares directly in an outcome, in predetermined proportions. Examples of commissions include:

- 1 percent of territory revenue

- 3 percent of territory gross margin

- 2 percent of revenue below sales quota plus 5 percent of revenue above sales quota

- $5 per unit sold

- 6 percent on category A products; 3 percent on category B products; 5 percent on equipment sales

The straight commission is the most entrepreneurial approach to sales force compensation. □

The straight commission is the most entrepreneurial approach to sales force compensation. As such, it is not surprising that straight commission is the preeminent approach to compensating *nonemployee* sales forces (distributors and manufacturer's reps).

Thus, in those highly entrepreneurial selling situations where the *employee* sales rep's role is comparable to that of the distributor rep (account allegiance being primarily to the sales rep, not to the company) it is logical to use a straight commission program. Classic straight commission sales positions are found in brokerage, commodities, real estate, and door-to-door sales.

The advantages of straight commission programs are:

■ Minimization of fixed employer cost

■ Ease of calculation and administration

■ Maximization of incentive to exceed

■ Attractiveness of unlimited earnings potential

The principal disadvantage of a straight commission program is the sacrifice of direction and control on the part of management. □

The principal disadvantage of a straight commission program is the sacrifice of direction and control on the part of management. From the recipient's point of view, the absence of secure income can also be viewed as a disadvantage. But, if the straight commission is being used in the optimum setting, for the highly entrepreneurial sales rep, then a minimum of management control is appropriate, and fluctuation in employee income, if severe, will be deserved.

The following situations indicate that a straight commission plan may be appropriate:

- The company is in an emerging industry or niche. Most competitors have lean, decentralized and dispersed sales resources.

- The company's competitive position is not strong. Financial resources are also limited.

- The sales role is highly focused on self-supervision and "closing." Few rewards are offered for effort of any kind that does not yield immediate sales results. Beyond stated policies and contract terms, each sales rep defines the job.

- The sales cycle is short. Success is realized quickly (or not at all).

- Barrier to entry is low.

The pure straight commission approach replicates the entrepreneurial experience. □

The pure straight commission approach replicates the entrepreneurial experience in that no guarantees (not even expense reimbursement) are offered. This approach enables a company to maximize the percent of income it can afford to share with the employee through commission, but at times can hinder recruiting or retention of qualified sales reps. Thus, straight commission plans are frequently accompanied by one or more of the following:

- Temporary guarantee

- Draw (recoverable or nonrecoverable)

- Expense reimbursement

Companies using a guarantee have to be sure not to extend the guarantee too long. □

A temporary guarantee recognizes that a sales rep may not achieve full effectiveness immediately (of course, if the position is truly a high prominence, straight commission job, the sales cycle is by definition short, so the guarantee should not last especially long). Typically, a guarantee states that for the first (for example) three months, the sales rep's total income will not be less than $X and for the next three months, not less than some lesser amount. Companies using a guarantee have to be sure not to extend the guarantee too long, thus protecting and retaining reps who will never reach an acceptable level of productivity.

A draw is an advance against future commission earnings, designed to neutralize income fluctuations somewhat. The net commission due will be the excess of accumulated commissions earned over accumulated draw payments. If draw payments exceed commissions after some point of time (usually at year-end), the rep may be required to return the excess to the company (a "recoverable" draw), or may be entitled to keep the excess (a "nonrecoverable" draw). Using a draw is quite common in straight commission programs, and can be helpful to a company in a variety of ways: facilitating recruiting, and eliminating (or at least reducing) complaints from the field about promptness of commission payments. As long as the draw is set at a level where deficits are unlikely (sometimes accomplished by establishing the maximum draw level at a percentage—e.g., 75 percent—of the prior year's earned commission), a draw usually benefits both the company and the commission sales rep.

Expense reimbursement for commission sales reps varies from no reimbursement to full reimbursement. □

Expense reimbursement for commission sales reps varies from no reimbursement (rep pays all expenses) to full reimbursement subject to company guidelines. Those companies reimbursing no expenses generally argue that they are directing the maximum resources possible to the commission rate itself; and the highly productive commission reps normally agree; they answer to no one but themselves (and

Most companies limit commission sales rep expense reimbursement to a "subsidy" rather than full reimbursement. □

the IRS) for their expenses, and are able to judge whether a particular outlay will have appropriate "payback" in commission income. While in theory the foregoing scenario is consistent with the entrepreneurial role, many companies do reimburse out-of-pocket expenses for commission reps, particularly mileage and hotel costs. This is done to ensure that the entire territory is covered, and to eliminate any financial disincentive the rep otherwise might have to cover distant accounts and prospects. Most companies, rightfully, limit commission sales rep expense reimbursement to a "subsidy" rather than full reimbursement, leaving to the rep to decide the reasonableness of the marginal dollar of outlay, weighing the cost against the profitable commission return. In this way, the commission sales rep remains, in effect, an independent business partner of the employer.

Combination Plans: Salary/ Commission (Low-Risk)

Many companies recognize that their sales roles do not fall completely at either end of the prominence spectrum; while the reps are not prototypical commission "peddlers," the company wishes to instill greater variance in compensation than is possible in salary-only programs. As a result, a significant percentage of American companies use a combination of salary and commission, trying to achieve the advantages of each.

A low-risk combination of salary and commission is sometimes referred to as "disguised base salary." Interestingly, the proportion of salary in the total cash package is sometimes quite low, giving the mistaken first impression of a risky, entrepreneurial program. For example, the plan might stipulate:

A low-risk combination of salary and commission is sometimes referred to as "disguised base salary." □

- Base salary, by grade, typical midpoint = $24,000

- Commission on all sales: 1 percent category A products; 1.5 percent category B products

- Quarterly maximum: 100 percent of base salary

Any combination of salary and commission which results in a predictable, stable income stream can be categorized as "disguised straight salary." Even in the ab-

Even in the absence of an explicit maximum on periodic earnings, a program can still fall under the "disguised salary" heading. □

sence of an explicit maximum on periodic earnings, a program can still fall under the "disguised salary" heading if:

■ The rate of commission decelerates after reaching a given level, e.g., 5 percent of sales up to 120 percent of quota plus 1 percent of sales above quota.

■ Incentives are expressed as a percentage of base salary, with a limit (explicit or practical) on earnings, e.g., 1 percent of salary for each 1 percent by which quota is exceeded up to 120 percent of quota, plus 0.2 percent of salary for each additional percent of quota realization.

Advantages of a low-risk "disguised straight salary" program include:

■ The ability to establish and administer sales-force salaries on a basis comparable to those of other company employees.

■ Control and predictability of commission expense.

■ Use of objective criteria to measure and reward differential sales performance.

■ Providing some incentive while maintaining the advantages of a straight salary program.

On the other hand, companies using low-risk programs sometimes find them disadvantageous:

- Sales reps can be discouraged from maximizing sales in a poor year, for fear that a significantly higher quota for future years will result.

- So much of the commission income is effectively assured (no territory will sell zero) that the actual percentage of pay truly at risk can become minuscule.

- Reps earning high-incentive may resist transfers or promotions to nonincentive eligible positions.

Salary and commission can be creatively combined to replicate the advantages of a straight commission program. □

A low-risk combination of salary and commission should be used only in selling situations in which:

- Prominence of the sales rep is low.

- The sales rep affects volume only indirectly; the combined impact of advertising, pricing, and promotions will have a "heavy" impact on success.

- The company product is recognized and the customer base is reasonably stable and loyal.

Combination Plans: Salary/ Commission (High-Risk)

Salary and commission can be creatively combined to replicate the advantages of a straight commission program, while still offering base salary sufficient to meet competitive requirements.

A high-risk "disguised straight commission" combination of salary and commission is characterized by one or more of the following features:

■ Part or all of base salary is treated as a guaranteed advance against incentive earnings.

■ A threshold or quota directly related to base salary must be met before commissions begin to be earned.

■ Base salaries are set at significantly below-market levels; therefore the entire determinant of the attainment of even average total earnings is the commission income earned.

Examples of formulas that operate as each of the three aforementioned disguised straight commissions are:

■ Base salary set according to experience (and prior sales volume); commissions paid at the rate of 6 percent of sales volume. Commissions are paid quarterly, net of base salary payments; for instance:

	Salary	Sales	Commission (6%)
Month 1	$ 4,000	$100,000	$ 6,000
Month 2	4,000	50,000	3,000
Month 3	4,000	60,000	3,600
Total	$12,000	$210,000	$12,600

Net commission due = $600 (normally, if there is a deficit it is carried forward and charged against future earned commissions).

Base salary is established based on territory potential. □

■ Base salary is established based on territory potential; a guideline is base salary should be set at 5 percent of sales quota—e.g., for a $1 million annual quota, a base salary of $50,000 would be paid. Commissions are paid at the rate of 5 percent for all sales above quota. Under this illustration (providing the quota is met or exceeded) the sales rep's income will be exactly the same as under a 5 percent straight commission plan.

■ Sales reps receive a $2,000 monthly base salary and are paid commissions on all sales; the "competitive" total cash range

Sales reps can feel a greater linkage to the company when a significant portion of total earnings is derived from a salary. □

for similar skills is $50,000–$100,000; in effect, the salary is incidental, since no qualified sales rep would be content to work for less than 50 percent of the low end of the competitive total cash range. The behavioral impact of this program will, therefore, be identical to that of a straight commission plan.

Advantages of "disguised commission" programs are:

■ Sales reps can feel a greater linkage to the company when a significant portion of total earnings is derived from a salary; salaries, even under disguised commission programs, have an aura of permanence and security that can be helpful in recruiting and retaining sales reps.

■ The allure of unlimited earnings potential, and the associated motivation, can be offered even in those situations where the "barrier to entry" is high, thus requiring significant base salary.

■ Having a salary component in the program enables the company to vary salary increases according to a more comprehensive set of performance criteria; under a straight commission program, no such mechanism is available, and sales reps frequently ignore all aspects of the job that do not lead quickly and directly to sales volume and commissions.

■ Differences in base salary can be neutralized more quickly than under a typical merit structure; total cash earnings can track closely with demonstrated productivity, since base salary is continually "validated" by sales results.

■ If earned commissions do not exceed the amounts "advanced" as salary, a strong negative performance message is delivered—namely, that unless productivity improves, the sales rep is not worth the existing base salary level; underachievers will often "get the message" and voluntarily begin to seek other employment.

Sales reps can be lured by competitors who offer a greater mix of base salary in the overall pay package. □

Disadvantages of disguised straight commission include:

■ Particularly in recessionary times, sales reps can be lured by competitors who offer a greater mix of base salary in the overall pay package.

■ Sales reps can ignore the salary portion of the compensation and their behavior may be driven strictly by whatever produces the quickest and easiest sale, ignoring those aspects (e.g., securing new accounts, introducing new products) of the job that take longer to achieve success.

A bonus may be defined as an opportunity to earn additional compensation by meeting a goal or series of goals. □

Increasingly, companies whose sales reps have a critical impact on volume but who nonetheless are paid high salaries have found the disguised commission alternative appealing. Market characteristics indicating that a disguised commission program could be optimum include:

- Sales reps have considerable impact on short-term volume results.

- The company perceives a need to energize a mature sales force that is already receiving competitive base salaries.

- Both the sales rep prominence in the marketing mix and the barrier to entry are high.

Combination Plans: Salary plus Bonus

The fifth of the five prevalent approaches of sales compensation is Salary plus Bonus.

A *bonus* may be defined as an *opportunity* to earn additional compensation by meeting a goal or series of goals. Bonuses are never the sole compensation mechanism; they are always paid *in addition to* base salary, never in lieu of salary. The bonus is the most flexible form of sales incentive compensation in that there is no limit to the goals that may be used.

Goals can be categorized as either:

■ *OBJECTIVE*—meaning there is observable *evidence* (not necessarily a revenue result, but an objective determination of whether or not the goal was achieved).

■ *SUBJECTIVE*—meaning that judgment is applied after the fact to determine the amount earned by a sales rep.

Subjectively determined bonuses have the obvious drawback of relying on after-the-fact judgments. □

Subjectively determined bonuses have the obvious drawback of relying on after-the-fact judgments, which may not always be viewed as fair. Far more importantly, however, subjective bonuses do not provide communication and direction *during the incentive period* of those important goals the company needs its sales force to accomplish. Arguably, all sales incentive programs are designed to reinforce the management process by *communicating* management's priorities, and therefore must contain *objective* performance goals and standards.

Within the objective family of measures, many permutations exist. Goals may be further subdivided into:

Volume Goals	Nonvolume Goals
Absolute volume	New account acquisition
Relative volume (to quota, to last year)	Key account accomplishments
	Product placements
Segmented volume (by product or channel)	Merchandising targets

Bonuses may be denominated in a number of different ways as well:

■ Percentage of base salary, e.g., 1 percent of base for each 1 percent increase in volume

■ Dollars, e.g., $1,000 for each qualifying new account

■ Points, e.g., 3 points per equipment sale; 3.8 points with service contract; value of a point = $100 if quota is met, $80 if not

Simply put, a bonus is one or more opportunities to earn additional compensation, based on the attainment of specified results. Ideally, the factors considered in the determination of the results meet the following criteria:

- Limited in number (3 to 5 maximum)

- Relevant and important

- Complete (sales rep cannot "afford" to ignore any important responsibility)

- Understandable

Advantages of bonus programs are numerous:

- Bonus plans provide flexibility in performance management.

- Marketing objectives can be translated into financial incentives.

- Rewards can be structured to recognize important selling *and* nonselling activities.

- Fixed costs are more limited and predictable.

- Base salary provides income stability while bonuses can offer sizeable earnings opportunities.

- A bonus plan lends itself to group (team, region, office) results more readily than a commission plan.

Disadvantages of the bonus approach include:

Bonus plans provide flexibility in performance management. □

■ The establishment and monitoring of goals requires strong sales and performance management.

■ Calculation and administration are more cumbersome than under salary or commission programs.

Volume is an incomplete indicator of sales effectiveness. □

Companies with some or all of the following market characteristics generally use a salary/bonus combination:

■ Sales force prominence is at neither extreme.

■ The sales cycle is long; important activities undertaken this quarter will not show up in this quarter's volume result.

■ Volume is an incomplete indicator of sales effectiveness.

■ Sales role varies significantly by customer segment. Therefore, only certain selected results are indicative of selling skills.

■ Management and sales reps, as a routine part of the management process, establish account and/or product-specific tasks and goals, which a bonus plan can reinforce.

- Sales teams, rather than individuals, are most directly responsible for overall sales results.

Regardless of which of the five approaches is used, a sales compensation program attempts to differentiate pay within the sales force on the basis of accomplishing difficult, controllable sales tasks. The program should be viewed as a "win-win" economic game, good for both the company and the sales rep; properly designed, the plan should provide above-market total cash compensation when (and only when) results indicate that a high level of selling skill has been used to help bring about important business results.

A sales compensation program attempts to differentiate pay within the sales force. □

Chapter 3

How Compensation Plans Can Drive Channel Sales

By John F. Tallitsch, Principal and National Practice Leader
Buck Consultants

Introduction

Due to the declining productivity of their companies' direct sales forces, suppliers' sales executives are under pressure to achieve significant performance results in the indirect sales channel. This occurs at a time when forces are reshaping supplier/customer relationships and share gains of end-user purchases have increased distributors'[1] "power" in the sales channel (see Table 3.1).

Complicating the situation is the tension that exists between suppliers and distributors. Suppliers complain that distributors don't give their products sufficient attention relative to the level of "investment" made directly and indirectly on behalf of distributors—e.g., market research, product positioning, product training, service support, advertising, joint sales calls. Distributors

---

[1] Hereafter, the term "distributor" refers to all the forms of independent business people who represent a supplier's products.

Table 3.1

Forces Reshaping Distribution Channel Dynamics

Change Agent	Impact on Selling Effort
Supplier Arbitrage	Reduction in the number of vendors from whom customers buy. Customers are trending toward master distributor arrangements.
Centralized Purchasing	Increased customer buying power. Bigger but less frequent deals. More, higher-level, and more sophisticated buying decision-makers.
Longer Sales Cycles	Elevated selling expenses due to the increased number of face-to-face (FTF) sales calls required to close deals and the rising cost of a FTF sales call.
Manufacturing and Logistics Strategies	Teaming between suppliers' and distributors' sales staffs and among distributors' sales representatives and suppliers' nonsales functions due to customers' desire for vendor involvement in the product design process and customers' raised standards for postsale service. Expanded investment in technology and plant and equipment to meet customers' JIT, TQM, and EDI requirements demands profit growth.
Weakening of the "Product Solution"	Blurring of product differences makes selling relationships key to competitive distinction. Selling applications, productivity- and cost-improvement solutions require deep knowledge of customers' businesses.
Heated Competition	Holding on to customers is critical. Price competition is less than gentlemanly. "Deep drilling" accounts with current and new products is more efficient and cost-effective than attempting to gain new customers or chalking up competitive "win-backs."

Table 3.1 continues

Table 3.1

(concluded)

Change Agent	Impact on Selling Effort
Distributors' Channel Power	Boosted influence in the channel reflects large distributors' market share expansions due to industry consolidation and customer appreciation of one-stop shopping, personalized but solutions-oriented selling, and value-added services. Higher distributor influence can potentially impact suppliers' manufacturing and selling economics.

complain that suppliers put their customer base at risk—e.g., stocking the channel with too many distributors, encouraging interproduct competition, placing employee sales representatives in direct competition with them. This mutual dissatisfaction exists because suppliers' historical channel management strategies and execution haven't accommodated the differences between suppliers' and distributors' business success formulas. There are fundamental differences in how each conducts its business. Suppliers pursue market share and profitability by maximizing product exposure through multiple channels. Distributors value profitability over market share and meet their goals by selling many suppliers' products to compara-

Suppliers pursue market share and profitability by maximizing product exposure. □

tively fewer customers. Suppliers create and make products. Until recently, many have not recognized the importance of providing superb service. Service quality has been, and will always be, a matter of life or death for distributors because products overlap across distributors.

Service quality has been, and will always be, a matter of life or death for distributors. □

In order to achieve heightened performance expectations, suppliers' sales executives must implement and successfully execute channel management strategies, including sales incentives, built around *both parties'* "wants" from the selling partnership—a "win-win" situation for suppliers and distributors (see Table 3.2).

Distributors enjoy substantial ability to exert control over the supplier in defining monetary and other business relationship terms in that their "ownership" of customers determines whether/how suppliers are aligned with end-users. In spite of distributors' channel power, suppliers can structure self-benefiting sales strategies and incentive arrangements because distributors' profit margins are pressured and price competition among distributors is heated and less than gentlemanly. Furthermore, going forward, distributors will be required to make substantial investments to satisfy customers' increasingly complex

Table 3.2

Supplier/Distributor Partnership "Wants"

Supplier "Wants" from Distributor	Productivity gains "Share of heart"—i.e., products foremost in distributor sales representatives' minds, proposed and effectively communicated to targeted customers in preferred markets Highly capable, tenured, product knowledgeable and "product advantage" selling sales force Feedback from the marketplace—e.g., product requirements, customer preferences, competitor actions
Distributor "Wants" from Supplier	Critical mass of profitable and fast-turning products Sales training—e.g., matched to customer needs, how to position the supplier's product relative to the competition, how to search out applications Timely communication—e.g., market and customer research/direction, new product and factory innovations, single point of contact Sales assistance—e.g., constructive joint sales calls on end-users, market research data, direct sales force matching functional support (order taking, technical problem solving, flexibility in handling requests, kept promises, merchandising, equitable policies) Attractive economics—i.e., commissions or functional discounts commensurate with the "creative salesmanship" required in light of the supplier's marketing mix weaknesses, supports that reduce distributor costs and/or "services," which command higher prices from customers

service demands. Therefore, "business as usual" is not a viable option for distributors.

Suppliers with a selling "blueprint" that has clear economic advantages for distributors, coupled with exciting, different, and competitive incentives and proactive channel management will be able to shift distributors' selling priorities. The end result will be greater revenue, profit, and share for suppliers.

Traditional incentive plans provide distributors with a commission or functional discount. □

Distributor Incentives

Traditional incentive plans provide distributors with a commission or functional discount, which may be fixed or variable (see Table 3.3).

Distributors are independent operators. They manage their businesses in a manner that advances their financial objectives. Traditional commission or functional discount arrangements reinforce this independence because they just reward distributors for making something happen—creating revenue or profit dollars for suppliers. Even with sufficient financial modeling to ensure end results are consistent with the supplier's financial objec-

Table 3.3

Type of Arrangement	Illustrative Incentive Format
Fixed Commission	Constant percent of total territory (or product) revenue or gross profit Uniform dollar amount per unit
Variable Commission	Commission percent or dollar per unit varies based on: • performance vs. prior year • quota percent attainment • level of aggregate volume or profit attained or size of individual sale • gross profit margin or percent to list price at which product is sold • type of product sold—new vs. "bread and butter" product

tives, such traditional incentives by themselves do not guarantee that distributors' results are secured through the market-penetrating selling behavior desired by suppliers. Questions remain unanswered. Did the revenue come from strategically important customers? Is the product mix balanced? How many targeted customers were introduced to the product? Suppliers that want to win, gain, and hold position within their target markets, and customers do care how and where distributors capture results. It is crucial, therefore, that suppliers implement incentive plans that encourage distributors to sell within the supplier's market penetration strategies. This is best accomplished through a combination of "traditional" and enhanced commissions or discounts. The former pays for "doing things right" while the latter spurs "doing the right things." These "right things" are depicted in the formula in Exhibit 3.1.

Performing well, or poorly, in one or more of the above factors can dramatically alter a supplier's share of its served market. Tables 3.4 and 3.5 illustrate how these market share drivers can be framed into a bonus plan aimed at stimulating distributor principals to direct their sales representatives to sell according to the supplier's "blueprint." Much of the data required to make this bonus plan work should be available in the supplier's order tracking system. Successful implementation requires enthusiastic communication of plan details, accurate tracking, and regular, face-to-face interaction between

Exhibit 3.1

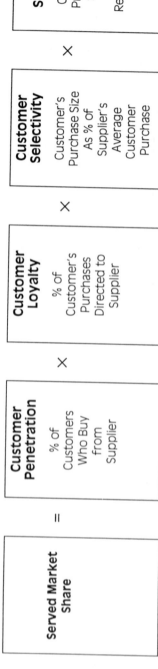

Served Market Share	=	Customer Penetration	×	Customer Loyalty	×	Customer Selectivity	×	Price Selectivity
		% of Customers Who Buy from Supplier		% of Customer's Purchases Directed to Supplier		Customer's Purchase Size As % of Supplier's Average Customer Purchase		Customer's Price as % of Supplier's Average Realized Price

Table 3.4   Conceptual Alternative #1

Performance Rating Instrument

Measure	Definition	Rating Scale	Score
Accounts Sold Ratio	# Accounts Sold ÷ # Potential Accounts[1]	0 2 4 6 8 10	
Revenue[2] per Account	Revenue ÷ # Accounts Sold	0 2 4 6 8 10	
New Accounts Sold[3]	# New Accounts Sold	0 2 4 6 8 10	
Revenue per New Account Sold	New Account Revenue ÷ # New Accounts Sold	0 2 4 6 8 10	
Order Size	Volume ÷ # Orders Written	0 2 4 6 8 10	
Priority Product Volume Mix	Priority Product Volume ÷ Aggregate Volume	0 2 4 6 8 10	
Target Accounts Sold	# Target Accounts Sold	0 2 4 6 8 10	
Revenue per Target Account	Target Account Revenue ÷ # Target Accounts Sold	0 2 4 6 8 10	
Quota Attainment	Aggregate Revenue ÷ Quota Revenue	0 2 4 6 8 10	
Average Revenue per Sales Rep[4]	Aggregate Revenue ÷ # Sales Reps	0 2 4 6 8 10	
		Total Score	
		Average Score	

(1) Potential accounts in territory. Ratio is a proxy for market penetration.

(2) Profit may be substituted for revenue throughout.

(3) New account is an account that hasn't purchased from the supplier, an account with volume < $X, and/or an account that hasn't purchased from the supplier in X years (a competitive "win back").

(4) The number or % of Sales Reps with revenue > $X could be substituted to drive performance improvement.

Table 3.5

Incentive Payout Schedule

Distributorship Performance Level		
Performance Level	**Average Rating Score**	**Principal's Bonus**
Below Minimum Acceptable	< 4	$0
Minimum Acceptable	4 to 5	$X
On Target	> 5 to 7	$X times 1.10
Excellent	> 7 to 8	$X times 1.15
Outstanding	> 8	$X times 1.25

the supplier's channel manager and the distributor principal or sales manager.

Exhibit 3.2 accentuates the strategic selling message that a supplier wants to convey to its distributors because the commission rate or functional discount swells (the "bump" effect) when the distributor performs well against targets that the supplier imposes for aggregate revenue, sales to "key" accounts, and performance in priority products. Executing well in all performance categories results in the most attractive rate. Low performance in one category can be offset with high production in an-

Exhibit 3.2   Conceptual Alternative #2

X% = Standard Commission Rate or Discount

Volume vs. Goal

YTD Goal Attainment	Commission or Discount Adjustment
95.1% to 100.0%	0.0%
100.1% to 105.0%	.05X%
105.1% to 110.0%	.10X%
110.1% and Above	.20X%

Weight = 50%

"Bump"

PLUS

Key Account Volume vs. Goal

YTD Goal Attainment	Commission or Discount Adjustment
95.1% to 100.0%	0.0%
100.1% to 105.0%	.025X%
105.1% to 110.0%	.05X%
110.1% and Above	.10X%

Weight = 25%

PLUS

Priority Products' Volume vs. Goal

YTD Goal Attainment	Commission or Discount Adjustment
95.1% to 100.0%	0.0%
100.1% to 105.0%	.025X%
105.1% to 110.0%	.05X%
110.1% and Above	10X%

Weight = 25%

other, producing an above-standard commission rate or discount.

Research by Bain & Co. in the Spring 1991 issue of *The National Productivity Review* indicates that providing the right incentives and matching distributor capability to end-user needs are critical for optimum market penetration. These findings provide valuable clues for suppliers as they create their distribution strategies. They can also be applied to distributor incentives. Consider the area of contests. Many suppliers utilize contests (through which distributor sales representatives and/or principals can earn awards or trips) as a means of encouraging distributors to improve their effectiveness in such non-volume criteria as business planning, financial management, marketing, and service capability expansion. The hope is that increased business effectiveness will translate into improved supplier results. Suppliers can heighten the importance of distributors' organizing for sales success, elevate their "power" in the distribution channel, and create further incentive payout discrimination among their distributors by linking contest results to distributors' commission rates or functional discounts.

Providing the right incentives and matching distributor capability to end-user needs are critical for optimum market penetration. □

Conceptual Alternative #3 in Table 3.6 creates a variable commission rate or functional discount based on the achievement of "Star Performer" status by the distributor in the supplier's annual contest. In *Conceptual Alternative #4* in Table 3.6, the distributorship's commission rate increases or its functional discount deepens based on sustaining "Star Performer" status over multiple years. Marrying contests and commission rates or functional discounts requires exact, demanding, and carefully calibrated performance criteria.

Table 3.6

Conceptual Alternative #3

Description: Achievement of "Star Performer" status enhances the distributor's commission rate or functional discount.

Example: The enhanced commission rate applicable to a "Star" distributorship would be 1.2 times the standard commission rate.

Conceptual Alternative #4

Description: Sustained "Star Performer" status magnifies the distributor's commission rate or functional discount. The distributor's failure to "renew" the "Star Performer" status in a year drops the commission rate or functional discount back down to the standard level for the next year and the "clock" starts all over again.

Example: The commission rate enhancement (as a multiple of the standard commission rate) for continuous years of "Star Performer" status is: 1 Year = 1.05X, 2 Years = 1.10X, 3 Years = 1.15X, 4 Years = 1.20X, 5 Years or more = 1.25X.

Otherwise, a supplier will end up paying twice for the same results—through the commission rate or functional discount and the contest. Finally, sophisticated measurement systems and personal ratings of distributor performance by the supplier's channel manager are required. Although a personal assessment of each distributor by the channel manager is time-consuming, the effort is worthwhile as it compels regular, constructive contact between the channel manager and distributor principal.

No distributor agreement or sales incentive, however effective, is an adequate substitute for "hands-on" channel management by suppliers. □

Channel Management Incentives

No distributor agreement or sales incentive, however effective, is an adequate substitute for "hands-on" channel management by suppliers. Suppliers should appoint a channel manager to represent their interests (objectives, strategies, and selling tactics) to distributors and relay distributors' "wants" back to them. This person should also have line accountability for the channel's performance. Accomplishing this task requires that the channel manager wear multiple hats and each of these channel management responsibilities should be considered in structuring incentives for this role. (See Table 3.7.)

Astute management of distributor roles and responsibilities as well as support programs can yield higher contribution margins than those realized in a supplier's direct channel. It is common that 80 percent of a supplier's revenue is generated by 20 percent of its customers—generally the supplier's large customers that are served by the direct channel. But, a supplier's administrative costs are driven by order quantity, not order size. And the vast majority of orders are likely to be initiated by smaller customers—typically, within the distributors' realm and channel manager's charge. By allocating the supplier's sales support resources according to distributor productivity, the channel manager can ensure that the supplier's cost to serve its distribution network doesn't escalate and disrupt this profit relationship.

A second key priority for the channel manager is the establishment of the supplier's "punch-counterpunch" capability. Sales objectives, strategies, and tactics can rapidly become outmoded because the importance of markets, products, and customers changes continuously. Fine-tuning of channel strategy and selling tactics on an

It is common that 80 percent of a supplier's revenue is generated by 20 percent of its customers. □

Table 3.7   Illustrative Roles and Responsibilities of Supplier's Channel Manager

Business counselor to distributor principal	Sales and marketing manager for distributors' sales forces	Distributor sales trainer (professional selling skills and product differentiating characteristics)
Gatherer of field-level market and customer intelligence from distributors	Provider of supplier-developed market intelligence to distributors	Arbitrator of special requests of supplier by distributors
"Air traffic controller" of supplier's support services to distributors and customers	Mediator of supplier's distribution channel policies to distributors	Evaluator of distributor and channel performance
Recruiter of new distributors	Peacemaker between supplier's product management functions competing for distributors' sales support	Creator/manager of supplier's "punch-counterpunch" capability

Both competitors and their threats will vary according to the challenges posed by the selling tactics of the supplier and its distributors. □

ongoing basis is necessary to ensure that the supplier and its distributors pursue the best opportunities. The channel manager should also view competitors from an offensive and defensive perspective. This is like a high-stakes chess game. The channel manager must determine offensive moves based on likely competitor reactions. Both competitors and their threats will vary according to the challenges posed by the selling tactics of the supplier and its distributors. And the channel manager's response to competitors' moves must consider the supplier's ability to deliver its counterpunch through independent distributors—another reason for treating distributors as allies in the sales channel rather than adversaries.

The third, and perhaps most important, imperative for the channel manager is the development and maintenance of distributor capabilities—e.g., business acumen, professional selling skills, recruiting and hiring, computer skills. Incremental profit, revenue, and share will be realized by the supplier that focuses on increasing the proportion of high capability distributors in its network.

Conventional channel management thinking drives the design of *Conceptual Alterna-*

tive #5 (see Exhibit 3.3). This thinking holds that it is difficult for suppliers to shift distributors' sales priorities from a product focus to a market segment orientation. However, *Conceptual Alternative #5* is flawed in spite of the fact that distributors have grown up by acquiring product lines. A key responsibility of the supplier's channel manager is to shift distributors away from a product focus and a "one size fits all" selling approach to customers. Linking the channel manager's incentive to aggregate revenue produced by the distribution network is not the best way to recognize the channel manager's effectiveness in supporting the distributor network and influencing different selling behaviors. At best, aggregating the revenue dilutes the importance—to the supplier and the channel manager—of selling strategically (e.g., focusing on key markets and high value customers). At worst, the importance of how and where revenue originates is ignored. A better incentive framework would be to segment the revenue, isolating those components that reflect the supplier's sales priorities *and* revealing the contribution made by the channel manager. Exhibit 3.4 is an example of such a plan.

A key responsibility of the supplier's channel manager is to shift distributors away from a product focus and a "one size fits all" approach to customers. □

Exhibit 3.3   Conceptual Alternative #5

Revenue Increment			Performance Level	Commission Rate on Revenue Increment	Commission Earned	
					Incremental	Cumulative
	Up to	$8,000,000	Below Minimum Acceptable	0.00%	$0	$0
$8,000,001	to	8,800,000	Minimum Acceptable	0.06%	5,000	5,000
8,800,001	to	9,680,000		0.80%	7,000	12,000
9,680,001	to	10,648,000	Target	0.83%	8,000	20,000
10,648,001	to	11,713,000	Excellent	0.94%	10,000	30,000
11,713,001	to	12,884,000		1.11%	13,000	43,000
12,884,001	to	14,172,000	Outstanding	1.32%	17,000	60,000
	over	14,172,000		1.41%		

Less than half of the channel manager's incentive opportunity in *Conceptual Alternative #6* in Exhibit 3.4 is tied to aggregate revenue. The majority is improvement-oriented, aligning the interests of the supplier and distributor. To earn an attractive incentive, the channel manager must know the "what" and "why" of distributors' past performance, develop a plan in support of distributors, and effectively marshal the appropriate supplier resources in support of distributors' efforts to capture improvement opportunities.

It may be appropriate to emphasize distributor capability over volume in [the] channel manager's incentive plan. □

For suppliers that are originating or building their distributor sales channel, it may be appropriate to emphasize distributor capability over volume in their channel manager's incentive plan. The priority reinforced in Exhibit 3.5 is the rapid growth of competencies—distributor capabilities *and* the supplier's internal sales support functions—needed to create competitive distinction in the marketplace. Revenue is included as an incentive component because the role of the channel manager includes signing up quality distributors and overseeing their sales efforts.

Exhibit 3.4 Conceptual Alternative #6

		Semiannual Incentive → Opportunity	Performance Minimum Acceptable Target Outstanding	Opportunity $3,000 $10,000 $30,000
Objective	**Aggregate Distributor Generated Revenue[1]**	**# of Distributorships with Revenue Growth > X%[2]**	**% of Customers Whose Purchases Have Grown by $X[3]**	**Growth in # of Customers Purchasing $X or More[2]**	**Customer Satisfaction Improvement[4]**
Performance Level Minimum Acceptable Target: Excellent: Outstanding:					
Objective and Incentive Weight	40%	20%	15%	15%	10%
Result					

Exhibit 3.4 continues

Exhibit 3.4 (Concluded)

Objective	Aggregate Distributor Generated Revenue[1]	# of Distributorships with Revenue Growth > X%[2]	% of Customers Whose Purchases Have Grown by $X[3]	Growth in # of Customers Purchasing $X or More[2]	Customer Satisfaction Improvement[4]
Performance Rating	Award Earnable for Performance Rating (At end of performance period, circle award amount earned for achievement vs. objective)[5]				
Below Minimum Acceptable	$ 0	$ 0	$ 0	$0	$0
Minimum Acceptable	1,200	600	450	450	300
Target	4,000	2,000	1,500	1,500	1,000
Excellent	7,200	3,600	2,700	2,700	1,800
Outstanding	12,000	6,000	4,500	4,500	3,000
				Total Award Earned	$

(1) For assigned distributorships

(2) YTD over prior year

(3) Measured by revenue

(4) Rating of distributorships supervised and supplier

(5) Award prorated for performance between levels

Exhibit 3.5

Conceptual Alternative #7

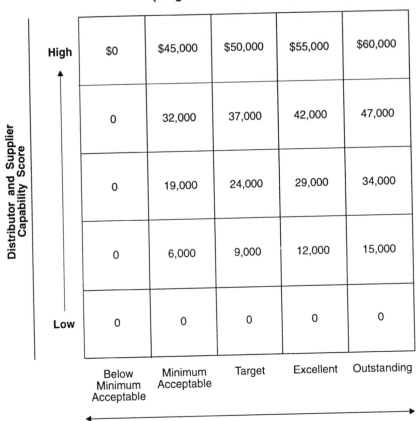

Annual Bonus Opportunity
(Weighted 3:1 toward Capability)

Distributor and Supplier Capability Score	Below Minimum Acceptable	Minimum Acceptable	Target	Excellent	Outstanding
High	$0	$45,000	$50,000	$55,000	$60,000
	0	32,000	37,000	42,000	47,000
	0	19,000	24,000	29,000	34,000
	0	6,000	9,000	12,000	15,000
Low	0	0	0	0	0

Aggregate Distributorship Revenue

Summary

Commissions on aggregate volume or functional discounts have traditionally been used by suppliers to compensate distributors because of the direct correlation between production and income. Suppliers found, however, that in implementing these schemes they traded away strategic selling control for plan design simplicity, the offer of unlimited earnings potential, etc. The challenge for sales executives is how to regain enough control in the sales channel so that they have a better chance of achieving the demanding productivity improvement goals set by senior management. Achieving this objective is akin to walking a tightrope. Too little control won't compel distributors to shift their selling approach toward the supplier's strategic selling "blueprint." Distributors' reaction to excessive control could be as extreme as denying suppliers access to customers. Creating distributor incentives that enable suppliers to achieve near- and longer-term selling objectives hinges upon identifying the selling behaviors that are strategically important to the supplier *and* understanding the key levers of revenue, cost, and profit for the distributor. Only in this way can incentives be designed that

Distributors' reaction to excessive control could be as extreme as denying suppliers access to customers. □

improve both parties' return on selling investment.

Chapter 4

Going beyond Volume

By Craig D. Ulrich, Principal
William M. Mercer, Incorporated

Introduction

The 1990s have so far provided much business upheaval and organizational change. With this change has come a fundamental shift in the role of many sales positions.

The role of the sales representative has become much more diverse than it was a decade ago. Today, the salesperson must balance a large number of responsibilities: managing the relationship with accounts, providing consultative advice on the application of the product or service sold, being the trouble-shooter for customer inquiries and complaints, and—not the least important—generating sales. Consultants have coined the term "consultative selling," but whatever the term used, the practical result is that the skills required and behaviors expected of today's sales representatives differ from those of their predecessors. Along with these different skills and behaviors have come different reward schemes to reinforce the application of these skills and behaviors.

This chapter will focus on those sales compensation schemes that reinforce the skillful execution of behaviors and responsibilities not directly connected with generating sales volume.

Sales Role Diversification

The most prominent behavioral change is a shift away from "push" selling. □

Two of the primary forces driving the role diversification and change for sales representatives are continuous quality improvement and technology. Both of these factors have had an instrumental effect on changing the role of salespeople.

The drive toward total quality exhibited by most U.S. companies has forced sales and marketing management to reassess not just the mix of behaviors necessary to perform the sales job, but also which behaviors lead to satisfied customers who continue to buy. The most prominent behavioral change is a shift away from "push" selling (i.e., push the features of the product or service at customers regardless of their specific needs) to "consultative" selling (i.e., the needs of the customer are assessed first and then a targeted application of a product or service is offered that matches the customer need). As might be presumed, the skills/knowledge/behaviors required of the sales representative operating under the new selling model is more advanced than what was required under the former model.

Since the salesperson is the primary, and sometimes only, contact point between the company and the customer, quality is often defined in the customer's mind by his or her relationship with the salesperson. The salesperson can strengthen or detract from the perceived quality of the product or service by how quickly and thoroughly he or she responds to customer inquiries, the skill with which he or she listens to and ferrets out the specific needs of the customer, and how well he or she balances the interests of the customer and those of the company.

Traditional sales compensation based solely on volume is no longer directly congruent with these skills and behaviors.

Technology has elevated the barriers to entry for a large number of sales positions. A decade ago, many sales jobs did not require a college degree—only good communications skills, drive and perseverance were important. Today, a bachelor of arts degree is often insufficient training to probe customers properly to determine

Technology has elevated the barriers to entry for a large number of sales positions. ☐

There is a substantive connection between the title changes and the knowledge and skills required of the new sales positions. □

their needs and then match these needs with a special application of the sales representative's products or services, particularly if the product or service is technology-based.

Even job titles have been adjusted to correspond with the new job requirements. In the high-technology community, we see the title Sales Engineer, while elsewhere the title Account Executive is used. Besides the universal desire to upgrade the status of all jobs, there is a substantive connection between the title changes and the knowledge and skills required of the new sales positions.

With this shift to more technically trained, more knowledgeable sales people comes the higher base salaries these individuals command.

Changes to Sales Compensation Schemes

Many sales and marketing executives are recognizing that commissions or incentives tied to sales volume need to be balanced with rewards for relationship management, customer satisfaction, profits, and various activity accomplishments. Experience has shown that volume alone does not ensure that other important factors in the selling equation are treated with sufficient attention, as evidenced by a common example.

A mid-size industrial company used the same sales compensation plan for eight years. The sales incentive scheme was solely volume-driven. In the past, when all of the products were similar in price and profit margin and the needs of the customers were fairly typical, the plan worked fine.

However, over the last two years, the company has expanded into new markets, launched three new products, and championed itself as a leader in quality.

At the close of the most recent fiscal year, the president questioned the vice-president of sales: "Why was the company experiencing turnover of its better sales representatives—the ones the customers uniformly respected and the ones who were constantly looked to by the other representatives for advice?"

After close examination, it became apparent that the three representatives who left were all faced with a myriad of responsibilities and more tasks than these individu-

Experience has shown that volume alone does not ensure that other important factors in the selling equation are treated with sufficient attention. ☐

als could possibly accomplish. These sales representatives were spending their time performing tasks that were leading to satisfied customers at the company's largest accounts as well as steady growth at these accounts, but these sales representatives were earning only average levels of compensation relative to their peers at the company. Since the incentive plan treated all sales representatives the same and paid only for growth in volume in their territory, these representatives were being penalized for how they spent their time. Although given the company's recent rate of attrition of accounts (i.e., 10 percent a year), and the fact that these representatives were securing and growing their company's large account foundation, they were being rewarded as if they had an immature territory with unlimited new business potential.

By developing a separate sales incentive plan for sales representatives responsible for large account management, the company was able to stem the turnover and better align the compensation plans to the specific sales roles.

Generally, incentives for accomplishment of activities other than generating volume tend to fall into two categories:

- Pay for Account Relationship/Customer Satisfaction

- Pay for Goal Achievement

Pay for Account Relationship

For reasons illustrated in the previous example, paying for account management and customer satisfaction can be a very wise investment for a company. Not every ounce of sales force energy needs to be directed at opening new markets and landing new accounts. Maintenance of core business with large and/or important accounts, particularly in a more saturated marketplace, is critical to success.

Maintenance of core business with large and/or important accounts is critical to success. □

In this regard, many companies are incorporating incentives for account maintenance and customer satisfaction into their reward schemes. The balance of this element vis-à-vis other elements is contingent upon the role of the sales representative, the profile of his or her accounts, and the sales strategies of the organization.

Two common variations of account management rewards are incentives for account retention and customer satisfaction.

The selection of either approach should be based on the characteristics of the selling job.

Account Retention

Providing incentives for account retention can be structured as either a reward for maintaining the account as a customer with a minimum sales volume throughout the year, or maintaining the total sales volume from existing accounts at a certain level.

Two common variations of account management rewards are incentives for account retention and customer satisfaction. □

The first arrangement is usually used for a sales representative who oversees a small to moderate number of large accounts. The latter approach is more often employed when a sales representative is responsible for a large number of accounts (i.e., 15 or more) in his or her territory.

A publishing company was experiencing solid growth in revenue and profits. However, the company's accounts were turning over at a 15 percent clip every year. An analysis of the company's accounts, its pricing, and its profit margins on all its products revealed that the growth was largely driven through price increases. More importantly, the terminated accounts were generally buying a larger volume of books at higher margins and the newer accounts were purchasing newer, lower-margin books. This company quietly realized that a few more years of this strategy was going to lead to disastrous results.

A significant change to the sales incentive plan was the introduction of an account maintenance incentive element, which rewarded sales representatives for holding sales attrition from existing accounts at 5 percent or less a year, regardless of new accounts generated. The incentive would grow if the volume from existing accounts improved from the 5 percent attrition threshold. A separate element was established for new account generation.

A significant change to the sales incentive plan was the introduction of an account maintenance incentive element. □

Customer Satisfaction

As the pronouncements from the quality gurus begin to fade a little, their message has provided a much needed push to sales and marketing management. Ten years ago, most attempts to measure quality and customer satisfaction would have resulted in some internally derived measure in which the actual customer would not participate directly.

Not only are top executives having a portion of their annual incentive tied to quality improvement or customer satisfaction, so too are sales professionals being tied to these measures. □

Times have changed. Not only are top executives having a portion of their annual incentive tied to quality improvement or customer satisfaction, so too are sales professionals being tied to these measures. From our experience, the thought of making this change often receives mixed reviews from sales and marketing management. However, for those organizations that have made the change, most are very pleased that they made the adjustment.

As with many incentive arrangements, there is no one "right answer" for incenting sales professionals for customer satisfaction. But essentially, there are two approaches.

One approach links the incentive award for customer satisfaction to overall sales volume. This approach structures the reward for customer satisfaction as a function of sales volume. See Exhibit 4.1 for an example of this design.

The other approach does not link customer satisfaction to sales volume. Instead, a relative measure of customer satisfaction is used.

With this approach, customer satisfaction is measured and compensated without consideration of sales volume.

Exhibit 4.1.

Sales Volume Attainment	Incentive Award
Sales Volume	
$ < $2 mil	$15,000
$2 – $3 mil	$20,000
> $3 mil	$25,000

X

Customer Satisfaction Performance Multiplier	Multiplier
Survey Rating	
< 85%	0.75
85% – 90%	1.00
> 90%	1.25

This particular design might look like this:

Performance Measure: Formal Survey

Measurement Period: Annual

Pay/Performance Arrangement.

Average Rating from Customers	Payout
Falls Short of Expectations	$0
Meets Expectations	$5,000
Exceeds Expectations	$10,000

Pay for Goal Achievement

Customer satisfaction is measured and compensated without consideration of sales volume. □

When examining the role of each sales position, the behaviors and attitudes connected with selling success, and the characteristics and factors shaping the market, we often find the prominence of the sales representative to be neither very low nor high. In these cases, rewarding strictly for volume is out of sync with what is truly required of the sales representative.

Instead, linking specific incentive payouts to the accomplishment of certain goals helps balance the need for overall sales volume growth with other accomplishments that are deemed critical to the success of the organization's sales strategy. Goals such as landing designated new accounts, making sales presentations to certain prospects in a new market, holding on to certain key accounts, and serving on a task force that launches a new sales information system are all worthy of consideration.

Sales compensation is a discipline in which there are few absolutes. □

Since sales compensation is a discipline in which there are few absolutes, many approaches will prove valid under the right circumstances. In the case of a sales representative whose prominence in the sales/marketing mix is moderate, the use of goal achievement incentives will often prove to be a wise choice.

A medium-size insurance company was struggling over the last five years with relatively flat sales growth. The company tried a number of different sales management strategies to boost sales growth, but significant change proved elusive.

The company's sales representatives were paid a flat commission on all sales above a certain threshold. For the most part, the company was able to renew its customers' policies each year at a rate of 93 percent. However, considerable time could be spent executing this responsibility, since policies were continually coming up for renewal throughout the year.

The commission rate for the sales representatives was tied to the growth in the book of business regardless of the size of the book. The company recognized that the representatives who were the most successful in building up a large book of business often were limited in obtaining new business due to the time commitments associated with renewal activities.

Therefore, to turbocharge new business while not disrupting the renewal process, the company undertook several changes. First, the company identified two different sales roles: one role was primarily new business development and the other focused largely on account management.

The business developers had their commission rate increased only for new sales, and an account management incentive scheme was developed to reinforce successful retention of a reduced number of customers. Based on the percent of accounts renewed, the sales representatives would earn relatively modest incentives, as shown below:

Retention	Payout
Below 85%	$0
85.0%–90.0% renewal	$5,000
90.1%–95.0% renewal	$10,000
95.1%–100% renewal	$20,000

With a low base salary, it became clear to these sales representatives that the bulk of their income was going to come from business development.

The other sales representatives had a somewhat similar incentive scheme, although with greater payout opportunity from account retention than from new business development.

Though this change took a little time to take hold, the organization began to experience the sales growth desired.

One-dimensional sales incentive schemes are insufficient to support today's more complex selling strategies. □

Pay for Profits

With the role of sales representatives becoming much more relationship oriented, many sales compensation plans are being redesigned to add or increase the emphasis on profits. This shift in plan design is resulting in sales compensation plans becoming more similar to incentives plans for General Managers.

Hardware and software companies are now finding themselves selling technology solutions rather than just products. □

The motivation behind this change is to encourage the sales representatives to think like business managers and not salespersons. Relationship oriented selling requires a much broader business perspective—a perspective which takes into account the needs of the customer across all the company's contact points.

An example of where this sales compensation program shift has taken place is the information technology industry. Many hardware and software companies are now finding themselves selling technology solutions rather than just products. This industry change has forced sales professionals to think and behave differently. Along with this behavior change has come an increasing use of profits as a preformance metric in their sales compensation plans.

As can be seen from the examples in this chapter, incentives for accomplishments other than volume provide the needed flexibility to reinforce the multifaceted sales roles found in many industries these days. Experience has shown that one-dimensional sales incentive schemes are insufficient to support today's more complex selling strategies.

Chapter 5

Rewarding for Customer Satisfaction: It Just Might Be a Good Idea

By Thomas R. Mott
National Practice Leader/Sales Compensation
Hewitt Associates LLC

Introduction

Every few years a potential sales compensation trend appears on the horizon. Sometimes it looms large, and sometimes it fades away. The latest is rewarding sales employees on the basis of measured customer satisfaction.

We begin by examining the Total Quality Management (TQM) movement's influence on human resource management in sales organizations, including an apparently growing interest in rewarding members of the sales force for their customer-satisfaction contributions. Then we focus on prevalence—how widespread is the practice of rewarding for measured customer satisfaction? Why is the practice not *more* widespread and what are the barriers or potential negatives? Next, we consider several company-specific factors that seem to support the practice in some organizations. Finally, we offer "how-to" thoughts—how to measure customer satisfaction, how to position it in the total framework of sales force rewards and recognition, and how to integrate measured customer satisfaction into an incentive program. This, then, is a subject that goes much deeper than "just" patching customer satisfaction measures on to existing sales incentive plans.

Total Quality Management is a commitment to becoming more focused on the satisfaction of customers and more successful in meeting their needs efficiently and profitably. □

Total Quality Management is, at its core, a commitment to becoming more focused on the satisfaction of customers and more successful in meeting their needs efficiently and profitably. The ways in which TQM has affected the management of corporate sales human resources vary by industry, but include these:

- Formation of account-specific teams for which the salesperson functions as account executive, "quarterbacking" others (who might be outside the sales department organizationally) to deepen and expand major customer relationships.

- Redefining some sales jobs into what might be called field "business managers" by increasing their accountability for strategic accomplishments and requiring more profit-conscious territory management.

- Establishing sales career progression steps and creating high-status "career" sales positions that encourage sales-people to remain in the field, thus building long-standing customer relationships. This contrasts with rotating the best salespeople into bigger (or supposedly "better") territories and ultimately promoting them to management.

- Focusing on sales process improvement, such as doing a better job of planning, submitting orders properly, working with customers to avoid stockouts or excess inventory, handling complaints effectively, and so forth.

- Involving salespeople more closely in important decisions that affect them— such as the design of their pay program.

- Rewarding salespeople more generously when important aspects of Total Quality are received, appreciated, and acknowledged by customers.

Of these six ways the TQM movement is affecting sales human resource management, five are widely accepted as "trends"; they are already solidly in place in many sales organizations. We are still waiting to see about the sixth—rewarding salespeople on the basis of measured customer satisfaction. Is it a solid trend? Is it a fad that will happen and die out? Is it mostly speculation and ivory tower conversation? We really cannot say; but the subject is getting serious attention because it just *might* be a great idea in certain situations.

Fewer than 7 percent said they use a customer satisfaction measure as one factor in determining field sales bonuses. □

How widespread is the practice of rewarding salespeople on the basis of customer satisfaction? The past two years Management Compensation Services (MCS), a division of Hewitt Associates, asked the more than 200 participants in its annual Sales Compensation Study whether they had explicitly integrated customer service or quality measures into their sales incentive programs. In 1993, 26 percent of those who answered said they had done something along these lines. Digging further into this data is enlightening.

■ When asked "If sales incentives are utilized, how are 1993 bonus payouts determined?" fewer than 7 percent said they use a customer satisfaction measure as one factor in determining field sales bonuses, and just 9 percent said they use it for field sales management. Yet, since 1991, the incidence of using customer satisfaction measures in incentive calculations has doubled for field sales positions and increased by over one-half in field sales management jobs.

■ Some of the approximately 7 percent that utilized customer survey satisfaction data for determining sales incentive payouts were (as were many other companies) also using surrogate measures—such as customer retention data, "internal" operational statistics (e.g., order accuracy), and completion of training programs designed to encourage customer service or quality. MBO-type objectives were used by 24 percent. Also, 16 percent used quality or customer service criteria in their *recognition* programs for sales employees.

In 1991, another survey of 81 companies known for leadership in "total quality" revealed that 24 percent of them used a formal customer satisfaction measure in their sales incentive compensation formula. Thirty-seven percent of these companies based their field sales salary adjustments partially on customer satisfaction.

It was reported early in 1994 that IBM has now decided to base 40 percent of its sales commission payouts on customers' satisfaction with their sales team, an unusually heavy emphasis on customer feedback. This is by a company that traditionally has relied heavily on sales compensation as a motivational tool, and has devoted a great deal of time and attention to the design of its sales compensation programs.

"Satisfaction is very tough to measure—we can't get our arms around it in an accurate, quantitative way." □

These data clearly indicate that *something* is going on. It may not be a groundswell, but it is at least serious experimentation reflecting genuine interest in the proposition of rewarding salespeople on the basis of measured customer satisfaction. At the same time, there are frequently cited impediments to installing reward and recognition programs based on customer satisfaction measures. These are:

- *Accuracy.* "Satisfaction is very tough to measure—we can't get our arms around it in an accurate, quantitative way."

- *Cost.* "I see how we *could* measure satisfaction, but it would take a huge commitment of time and money to put the necessary systems in place."

- *Fairness.* "Customers' satisfaction with 'us' as a company is measurable, but how can we factor out customer attitudes toward those things the salesperson *doesn't* influence (such as our product quality) in order to reward just those customer satisfaction elements he or she *can* influence."

- *Redundancy.* "Satisfied customers buy more, quibble less about price and terms, and stick with us rather than shop competitive vendors periodically. We should simply base sales incentive compensation on sales volume, gross margins, and customer retention—because only by satisfying customers will a salesperson win under all three of these measures."

There is always a reliable way to measure customer satisfaction if there is a strong enough determination to do it. □

The first two of the preceding four arguments are refutable. There is always a reliable way to measure customer satisfaction if there is a strong enough determination to do it. And the cost of listening to customers, in relation to the benefits, is usually viewed as a very sound investment by those businesspeople who are seriously pursuing long-term success strategies. The third reservation (factoring out the uncontrollables) requires careful process design, but it can be overcome. One company, for example, used only *one* summary "check-the-box" score from customers as input into each salesperson's incentive plan payout. However, eight other "check-the-box" set-up questions that preceded it focused

Declining order volume, customer demands for greater discounts, and defections to other suppliers are consequences of deteriorating customer satisfaction. □

the survey respondent on those specific things the salesperson clearly controlled, not "general" company factors. The set-up questions (which were created with the help of the salespeople themselves), together with very clear instructions to the surveyed customers about the specific purpose of the rating tool, got this company smoothly beyond this issue in a way that was accepted by the field.

Consider the fourth argument, the one about redundancy with the more traditional sales performance and reward factors. No doubt there *is* correlation between customer satisfaction and more traditional factors of sales performance such as volume, margins, and customer retention. However (and this is important), declining order volume, customer demands for greater discounts, and defections to other suppliers are consequences of deteriorating customer satisfaction. They are "lag" indicators, whereas customers' satisfaction is a leading indicator of volume, margins, and account retention—just as help-wanted advertising lineage is a leading indicator of a stronger economy, whereas the unemployment rate is a lag indicator. Thus, measuring and rewarding customer satisfaction might be viewed as a form of "preventive medicine."

Why would a company decide to pay on the basis of customer satisfaction achievement? The economic consequence of losing current customers is becoming of greater concern to more business leaders. The American Management Association's research has concluded it is five to six times more expensive to acquire a new customer than to keep one. Some would argue this statistic alone suggests that serious resources should be devoted to sensing customer satisfaction and rewarding it when it happens, but there are at least two other factors that seem to prompt companies to reward salespeople on customer satisfaction. The first factor is present when the company adopts an organization-wide commitment to improving levels of customer satisfaction.[1] In these environments, *executives* are rewarded for it, customer service people are rewarded for it, and broad-based employee group incentive programs might even include it as a factor. The second prompt occurs when the particular sales role lends itself to rewarding customer satisfaction. In this regard, we have identified several tests to apply to

It is five to six times more expensive to acquire a new customer than to keep one. □

---

1 Jack Welch, GE's CEO and Chairman, has said, "The three most important things you need to measure in a business are customer satisfaction, employee satisfaction, and cash flow."

sales jobs; "yes" answers by a company to the following questions would provide support for rewarding its sales force based on customer satisfaction.

- *Repurchasing.* Is the selling process one in which the skills, attitudes, and training of the salesperson greatly affect whether customers will repurchase—or whether customers will provide a favorable reference when asked?

- *Postsale Relationships.* Does the salesperson serve as the critical point of contact with customers after the initial sale to provide ongoing services, technical solutions, product application ideas, etc.?

- *Account Team Concept.* Does the salesperson coordinate a team of specialists that is devoted to providing a range of services to one or more key customers?

- *Concentration of Sales Revenue.* Is the salesperson responsible for one or more very large key accounts that comprise a substantial percentage (e.g., 3 percent or more) of the company's or the division's ongoing revenue stream?

When both factors (widespread company commitment and appropriate sales role definition) appear simultaneously in a company environment, an argument for rewarding salespeople in that organization based on customer satisfaction can become extremely powerful.

How should customer satisfaction be measured? Ask customers to tell you how satisfied they are—it's that simple. Of course, there are serious issues of creating the proper data collection instrument, validating the process, and obtaining an appropriate sample, but these are issues competent marketing researchers have worked through for decades. Measuring customer satisfaction *is* indeed a science, but it is *not* "rocket science."

Measuring customer satisfaction is indeed a science, but it is not "rocket science." □

Without exception, it always seems a good idea to involve customers through interviews or focus groups in the process of deciding which of the salesperson's many deliverables are important enough to be measured. One company used this process to develop these customer satisfaction factors, which then were defined and surveyed using an appropriate rating scale:

- Frequency of contact by salesperson
- Timeliness of response by salesperson
- Product knowledge and the ability to provide comparisons with competitive products
- Quality of technical assistance provided

- Coordination of resources

- Initiative in suggesting new ideas

Each company must discover its own factors for defining customer satisfaction. □

Each company, of course, must discover its own factors for defining customer satisfaction based on the sales role, the nature of its customers, and those customers' expectations.

For organizations that believe their customers may be unwilling to be surveyed or feel they will resent being asked, there are alternatives to surveying customers about their satisfaction. Usually this means relying on operational measures. For example, after customer focus groups identify what sales force deliverables are important to them (such as call frequency, order accuracy, etc.), the company can attempt to measure and/or evaluate these items throughout the sales force. However, customers' expectations are dynamic, so the operating measures that are selected as "surrogates for customer satisfaction" may not remain appropriate over time, and measurement of many of them is certainly going to be imperfect. Thus, it is relatively natural for members of a sales organization to have reservations about using this kind of process to gauge customer satisfaction.

It is necessary to consider precisely where, in the overall framework of sales compensation, customer satisfaction should be recognized and rewarded. There is no "one right answer" to this question, but we can offer one tool that may be helpful in thinking about it, the "Total Sales Compensation Framework" (Exhibit 5.1). It illustrates seven alternative reward and recognition vehicles, some cash, some noncash, some immediate, some medium-term, and some long-term. These are not mutually exclusive. For example, the following combinations would work:

It is necessary to consider precisely where, in the overall framework of sales compensation, customer satisfaction should be recognized and rewarded. □

- *Commission and Recognition.* In a particular company, customer service excellence might be given an "immediacy" by having commission rates that vary according to the previous period's customer satisfaction achievement, while also being recognized over a longer period by inclusion as a key ingredient in membership selection standards for the organization (e.g., "President's Club") that is reserved for the sales organization's role models.

- *Salary Review and Promotion.* Customer satisfaction might be a standard factor in the sales organization's formal performance evaluation process, thus affecting

Exhibit 5.1   Total Sales Compensation Framework

	Immediate/ Short-Term	Sustained/ Medium-Term	Ongoing/ Longer-Term
Cash	**Commission:** For more immediate sale-by-sale or day-by-day results; often volume-oriented.	**Bonus:** For more measurable goal-oriented aspects of performance that require consistent reinforcement; often strategic.	**Salary/Performance Evaluation:** For less quantifiable (the "how") aspects of performance; things that foster long-term company success. **Long-Term Incentives (e.g., Stock Options):** For sustained performance and long-term loyalty ("handcuffs").
Noncash	**Contests:** For temporary priorities and action items that require "hype" in order to attract attention.	**Recognition:** For distinguished or "role model" performance on all aspects of the job.	**Promotion/Advancement:** For sustained high performance and for demonstrated capability to accept greater responsibility.

merit salary increases, while also being a key consideration in deciding who should be promoted into "account executive" status or into sales management.

Assume a company decides to incorporate a "hard" measure of customer satisfaction into its sales incentive calculations. What are the ways this can be done? The first aspect of this answer is "linked" or "unlinked." In an unlinked design, the payout for customer satisfaction takes the form of a simple bonus opportunity that is independent of other features of the incentive plan. This is a direct and straightforward approach, but it may not be optimal if it creates the perception that customer satisfaction has become a small "add-on" or "afterthought" in the incentive plan. Experience suggests that a small factor in the incentive plan (i.e., one that accounts for less than one-fifth of the total payout) might become lost if presented as an unlinked earnings opportunity.

Customer satisfaction might be a standard factor in the sales organization's formal performance evaluation process. □

Explicitly linking the customer service component to other payout factors can, on the other hand, "leverage" its importance, sending a message that customer satisfaction is an integral and important feature of the incentive program. Some illustrations of how linkage could be done follow:

Explicitly linking the customer service component to other payout factors can "leverage" its importance. □

- *Multiplier.* Make customer satisfaction a multiplier on the commissions earned (i.e., the multiplier value changes in direct relation to a customer satisfaction measure) or offer a higher commission rate during the upcoming performance period based on measured customer service performance in the prior period.

- *Matrix.* Put a customer satisfaction measure on the vertical axis of a bonus matrix, where the horizontal axis represents a "competing" variable such as new account acquisition. In this kind of design, the higher bonus amounts are paid for balanced performance in the upper right-hand corner of the matrix—lots of new customers and very satisfied current customers.

- *Hurdles.* Specify a threshold level of customer satisfaction as a hurdle that must be exceeded in order to receive some other element or portion of the incentive package; perhaps offer a corresponding "kicker" on the upside to reward those who maintain unusually high customer satisfaction ratings over an extended period.

The possibilities for incorporating customer satisfaction into incentive design are virtually endless—but imagination and creativity must be balanced with the goal of simplicity in design and administration.

Ten years from now, will we still be talking about the importance of customer satisfaction? Surely. About techniques for its measurement? Definitely. About paying salespeople based on those measures? That's a good question. The movement toward rewarding customer satisfaction will probably continue, at least in a gradual way, but stop somewhere short of being a standard feature in sales compensation plans. It will likely become more common, but not uniform, among jobs that pass the "tests" outlined in this chapter.

The possibilities for incorporating customer satisfaction into incentive design are virtually endless. □

Chapter 6

Rewarding Team Sales

By Maureen A. Meisner, Senior Consultant
Sibson & Company

Introduction

Team selling is everywhere. Be it spark plugs, insurance policies, or turbines, the team selling approach is steadily growing in popularity as companies strive to find new ways to differentiate themselves and their products from their competitors.

The reason is simple. Today's team approach to selling is centered on changing and increasingly individualized and complex customer needs—needs that frequently cannot be met by individual salespeople. Like their selling counterparts, today's buyers are more sophisticated as they manage toward the achievement of specific strategies and aggressive financial objectives. As the cost of purchasing can far outweigh the supplier's cost of selling, many companies want more from their suppliers than a series of transactions. Customers are now looking to forge value-added relationships.

As a result of these continually changing customer needs and expectations, the evolution of team selling has remained dynamic. "First generation" selling teams were generally made up

With the proliferation of similar products in the marketplace, differentiation now comes from the offering surrounding the product. □

exclusively of sales reps organized around a product or by geography. However, now, companies as diverse as R.R. Donnelley, Nestlé, and Allstate, to name a few, have discovered that improving and perfecting the overall customer interface now requires a team approach that draws on many of the company's resources—from product design to logistics to finance. The fact is, companies are facing a marketplace with a broader array of customer needs than ever before, which a superior product alone will not satisfy—but that a team of integrated resources can. See the appendix at the end of this chapter for a discussion of the different types of team members.

With the proliferation of similar products in the marketplace, differentiation now comes from the *offering* surrounding the product—that is, company- or industry-specific customization, service, pricing, delivery, installation, turnaround time, and so on. As the gap between the product and the offering widens, as shown in Exhibit 6.1, the product itself is reduced almost to the status of a commodity.

A company's competitive advantage now lies in its ability to leverage its internal resources to develop a superior product *offering* that meets the customer's require-

Exhibit 6.1

The Product/Offering Evolution

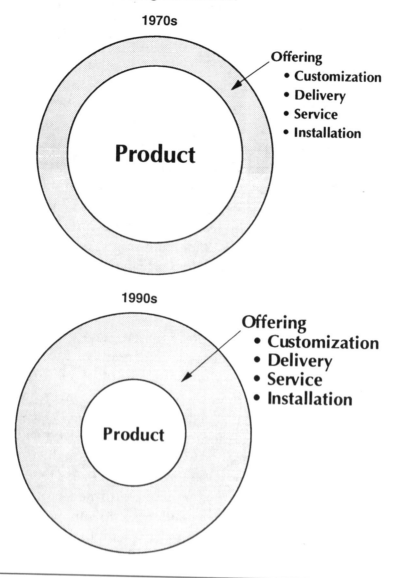

Understanding and managing the varied intricacies of the offering are changing the face of traditional buying and selling. □

ments. For example, at one time, software companies competed by selling generic database software. Now, with a glut of those packages on the market, these companies have had no choice but to expand the product offering to meet the specific needs of a particular company or industry. Hospitals that want a faster and less paper-intensive approach to file for Medicare reimbursement now demand a customized database software package that will adequately fill that need. And when payment for the product is conditioned on the system being up and "accepted," the role of certain team members becomes very clear. Clearly, understanding and managing the varied intricacies of the offering are changing the face of traditional buying and selling.

The question is, then, how do firms provide adequate and relevant incentives to such a diverse group of people? More to the point, what exactly is a team? Selling "teams" exist in virtually every organization, but may not be recognized as teams either by label or organizationally through team-based incentives. It's easy to see why. These teams may be formed on an informal, as-needed basis to satisfy customer needs, making it difficult to plug them into a traditional team-based reward system.

Yet, it is precisely the integral role these teams play in satisfying customer needs that makes recognition of their contributions to the company's success so critical. When designed properly, such reward systems provide the necessary incentives to focus team members and the entire organization on those activities that are most valued by the customer.

Selling "teams" exist in virtually every organization, but may not be formally recognized as teams. □

Designing incentives for selling teams—no matter how complex—addresses four key issues:

1. Who is a team member?

2. How will their performance be measured?

3. What will be rewarded?

4. How will team performance rewards be delivered?

Step 1: Who Is a Team Member?

Many individuals within the seller's organization "touch" customers in some way. However, it is important to understand which positions add value in significant *and* measurable ways before adding them to the team. Oversubscribing team

The number and types of jobs on a selling team may vary from product to product and from company to company. □

membership can lead to loose accountability and may mask other organizational shortcomings.

For example, a major manufacturer wanted to include accounts receivable reps on the sales team because these individuals deal with customers frequently. However, the need for this interaction usually resulted from the customer's inability to get a useful answer from the sales rep. In this case, the company wanted to base sales team membership not on a customer need, but on a flaw in the sales organization. On the other hand, if the company's accounts receivable function takes the lead in developing special billing or credit arrangements with customers directly, then accounts receivable should be considered for team membership.

There is no pat formula for determining who is a member of a selling team and, therefore, eligible for team-based incentives. The number and types of jobs on a selling team may vary from product to product and from company to company. So, when deciding who should be considered part of the team, the primary question to ask is, who is responsible for activities that the customer values? The short answer is that someone should be considered a team member if his or her contributions are recognized as valuable by customers, *not* by what is dictated by the organization. Unfortunately, many companies that adopt a team selling approach have been unsuccessful because they have formed teams according to the dictates of the existing incentive plan or the organizational structure.

Meeting Customer Needs

Teams should exist, operate, and be rewarded to satisfy customer needs. Because these needs are constantly evolving, the limitations of a traditional functional approach may fail to meet important customer requirements. It is critical to talk to buyers, understand their strategies and objectives—even how they are rewarded—and then determine what configuration of resources can best deliver results. This may mean different team configurations for different products, markets, or customers that change frequently over time.

Teams should exist, operate, and be rewarded to satisfy customer needs. □

The point is that *any* function in the organization has a place on a selling team, *as long as it contributes to or fulfills a critical customer need.* Over time, selling teams have evolved in response to discrete customer requirements. A few such examples are

Any function in the organization has a place on a selling team, as long as it contributes to or fulfills a critical customer need. □

illustrated in Table 6.1. Any one customer, market, or product may have one or a combination of customer needs. For example, if a customer requires a supplier to provide the capacity for multiple location purchasing, inventory management, and special billing and credit arrangements, the selling team may be made up of national and local sales reps, expediters, and accounting personnel.

Adding Value to the Customer

The next step in this process is to determine who adds value to the customer relationship and how. Using interviews with customers, customer surveys, and/or input from the field organization, companies can identify the key sales and service activities that help manage, develop, and support the offering and determine how the customer values each one of those activities. The results of the diagnostic tool depicted in Exhibit 6.2 can help indicate which jobs have a rightful place on the selling team, and lay the groundwork for determining what activities to reward and how to reward them.

If the accountabilities of a particular job cluster around two or more value-added

Table 6.1

Predominant Customer Need	Possible Team Members
Multiple location purchasing requirements	National/local sales reps, billing
Highly technical product customization	Sales, engineering, marketing
Education on product/service use	Sales, customer service
Inventory management	Sales, expediters, billing
Billing and credit arrangements	Sales, accounting
Industry expertise/application	Product/industry reps

activities, include several shared account-abilities, or drive a high proportion of value-added activities, then the job has a place on the team and should be measured as such. A position drives a specific process if it has the lead role and accountability for ensuring high-quality execution of that activity. Positions that influence the process generally provide key information for or support to that activity. So based on the example shown in Exhibit 6.2, the selling team should be comprised of sales reps, sales engineers, and marketing reps. Warehousing and delivery personnel may also be candidates for the team.

Positions that drive a process have lead accountability for ensuring high quality execution. □

Exhibit 6.2   Who's on the Sales Team?

Sales/Service Activities	Value to Customer	Direct Sales	Telemar-keting	Customer Service	Sales Engineer	Acct'g/Billing	Warehouse & Delivery	Marketing
MANAGE OFFERING								
• Lead Identification	Low		D					I
• Lead Qualification	Low	I	D					I
• Capability Demonstration	High	D			D			I
• Relationship Management	Medium to High	D						
DEVELOP OFFERING								
• Product Application	High	D			I			I
• Product Specifications	High				D			
• Bill of Materials	Medium				D		I	
• Pricing/Contracts	High	D			I	I		

Exhibit 6.2 continues

Exhibit 6.2 (Concluded)

Sales/Service Activities	Value to Customer	Direct Sales	Telemarketing	Customer Service	Sales Engineer	Acct'g/ Billing	Warehouse & Delivery	Marketing
				SUPPORT OFFERING				
• Product Delivery/Installation	High	I			I		D	
• Product Status (availability)	Medium			I			D	
• Product Training	Low	I			D			
• Credit/Billing	High	I				D		
• Product Enhancements/Updates	Low	I		I	D			
• Customer Complaints/Inquiries	High	I		D	I	I	I	I

Key

D = Drives the process

I = Influences or provides information to process

Setting Up Effective Teams

It is critical to identify and eliminate the barriers to effective communication and collaboration. □

Once the company has identified important customer requirements and who in the organization drives those responsibilities, it must set up teams that work effectively—that is, teams that are fully supported by the management, culture, and communication and administrative systems of the organization. By definition, teams are meant to operate with less hierarchy and greater empowerment, rendering traditional structures, job descriptions, and compensation ineffective. Therefore, it is critical to identify and eliminate the barriers to effective communication and collaboration. And these may mean changes more far-reaching than the sales organization. For example, a selling organization that needed shorter turnaround on design sketches was also experiencing considerable friction between its sales force and its sales engineers. By requiring that each sales engineer make one sales call per quarter with the sales rep and that sales reps themselves "spec out" one proposal per year (with coaching from sales engineering), clearer communication was established and turnaround time improved. The overall result was that sales engineering had a better sense of what was important to the customer and the sales force had a better understanding of the engineering implications of customer requests.

Step 2: What Do You Measure?

Once the makeup of the team has been established, the next step in designing team-based rewards is to determine what results the program should measure. The key to rewarding team-based selling is to focus on those measures that are most valued by the customer (e.g., industry expertise, inventory management, pricing, quality, etc.) *balanced* with the strategic business objectives of the selling organization (e.g., revenue, profit, market share, customer penetration, strategic product mix, etc.). The point is, team incentives can't be designed in a vacuum. They must be carefully planned to consider the company's overall strategic objectives. After all, a company will gain little by measuring inventory management if such a measure undercuts one of its strategic objectives, like overall profitability. Using Exhibit 6.3, a company can take the customer analysis a step further and begin to determine how customer value-added activities align with important company goals.

The key to rewarding team-based selling is to focus on those measures that are most valued by the customer. □

Exhibit 6.3

Developing Appropriate Measures

Sales/Service Activities	Value to Customer (1 to 10)	Linkage to Business Plan Goals (1 to 10)	Overall Score[1]
1. Lead Identification	1	7	4
2. Lead Qualification	2	9	5.5
3. Capabilities Demonstration	9	7	8
4. Relationship Management	7	9	8
5. Product Application	10	8	9
6. Product Specifications	9	6	7.5
7. Bill of Materials	6	6	6
8. Pricing/Contracts	10	9	9.5
9. Product Delivery/Installation	10	7	8.5
10. Product Status (availability)	7	9	8
11. Product Training	3	5	4
12. Credit/Billing	8	8	8
13. Product Enhancements/ Updates	3	5	4
14. Response to Customer Inquiries/Complaints	9	7	8

Key

1–3   =   Low Value-Added

7–10 =   High Value-Added

[1] Each score weighted 50%.

As shown here, several activities clearly should be measures of performance based on their high rankings with regard to both customer value and the business plan. For example, response to customer inquiries or complaints is of high importance to customers, as well as to the success of the business plan. To improve response time, a company may choose to measure improvement over current levels or relative to industry benchmarks. However, if response time is the leading indicator of customer retention, improvement in retention levels may represent a more comprehensive measure. Responsiveness may also correlate highly with subsequent sales orders and, therefore, directly influence customer penetration. The challenge is to make these distinctions and prioritize key measures to drive the incentive plan and to maximize the measures' coverage of objectives while minimizing redundancy.

The challenge is to maximize the measures' coverage of objectives while minimizing redundancies. ☐

In addition to supporting the needs of both the business plan and customers, the types of performance to measure and reward should:

- Ensure that team members have the appropriate resources and decision-making authority to achieve the performance result.

■ Establish standards of expected performance that are "quantifiable" in numerical or other terms (e.g., milestones of performance). These standards may reflect business plan, customer, or industry benchmarks.

■ Ensure that each performance result or a meaningful milestone toward that performance result is attainable within a stated performance period.

■ Ensure that methods for tracking, reporting, and assessing performance are readily available.

Measures and rewards should be limited to performance that employees significantly influence. □

When measuring team members' contributions, the incentive program must also have provisions to consider factors beyond team members' control, such as suppliers that deliver parts late and hold up an order. After all, no one has total control over everything, so measures and rewards should be limited to performance that employees significantly influence. In general, performance measurement is taken in aggregate to minimize the impact of a few nonrepresentative experiences. An exception to this rule is a team member who works with a large account, such as a large retailer, and has a single measure for that particular customer.

Step 3: What Should You Pay For?

By now, there will be a whole universe of activities and results to measure, but only a few select measures (generally *not more than two or three*) should be the basis for team member rewards. If the pay plan has more than three measures, the participant will reduce the number of measures in practice by ignoring some and combining others. The selected measures should be weighted to reflect their relative importance in the achievement of overall business and customer results. However, no single measure should account for less than 10 percent of a team member's total cash compensation, also known as the "rule of 10." Incentives set below this level generally fail to catch the attention or change the behavior of the team member. But this does not preclude members from participating in incentive compensation at levels that reflect their level of influence or prominence in achieving performance results.

Any measure that is rewarded in the incentive plan must help drive the financial success of the organization. It is critical to ensure that measures intended to drive positive financial results don't in practice

If the pay plan has more than three measures, the participant will reduce the number of measures in practice by ignoring some and combining others. ☐

actually harm the organization. For example, by measuring sales volume, a company may inadvertently encourage indiscriminate selling without accountability for profitability, so rewarding profitability or expense management may be a better alternative. Although profit is almost always an intrinsically good measure for rewards, other measures, such as margin, may not be. In one sales organization, a sales team was eligible for incentives if the team met certain margin goals. As a result, some team members refused to write business that did not meet minimum margin levels despite having long-term relationships with those customers.

Measuring Progress

Any measure that *indicates progress* toward an overall result generally is not included when determining rewards. The exception is when, in extreme situations, people in the organization simply will not do certain activities unless they are paid to do them. Generally, in these situations, rewards are only temporary (not more than one year) until the situation is rectified. For example, if a company's accounts receivable cost is escalating because of the increasing number of delinquent accounts, the near-term solution may be to use incentives to reduce the number of delinquent accounts through better customer qualification and more strict credit terms. Not coincidentally, these are activities the sales team can influence directly. Over the longer term, however, these activities should become a part of the overall job and should not be rewarded directly.

Contribute to Results

Measures that *contribute to or are secondary to a desired result* should also be examined carefully. These measures may be used to reward key players or to screen out extraneous factors. For example, if team members control product pricing but not the fluctuating cost of materials, the measurement of bottom-line profit may be inappropriate.

If team members control product pricing but not the fluctuating cost of materials, the measurement of bottom-line profit may be inappropriate. □

Drive Key Financial Results

Measures based on key financial results are prime territory for reward determination. As a general rule, these payouts should not be overly long-term, say, more than two years, and team members should have significant input or influence on their outcome. For example, an insurance com-

Measures based on key financial results are prime territory for reward determination. □

pany holds field/headquarters teams responsible for loss ratio (sales profitability) because each member plays a different, yet integral, role in delivering a lower loss ratio to the company. Field reps manage loss ratio by better up-front qualification of customers, while headquarters manages loss ratio through better pricing (i.e., underwriting) and appropriate expense management.

The bottom line is that any measure linked directly to reward determination should also be linked to the business plan and have direct influence on customer satisfaction and the perceived value of the product. The chart in Exhibit 6.4 can help categorize each performance measure and identify those measures that are top candidates for reward purposes.

Determine the Level of Measure

Beyond choosing appropriate measurement criteria, it is critical to specify the level (i.e., company, business unit, region, territory, etc.) at which performance will be measured, or the weighting across multiple levels. Generally, measuring performance at the most "local" level is preferred or weighted the greatest to reflect

Exhibit 6.4

What to Pay For

Sales/Service Accountabilities	Alternative Measures	Measure Assessment		
		Indicates Progress	Contributory or Secondary Results	Results
1. Pricing/Contracts	● Revenue		✓	
	● Margin		✓	
	● Profit			✓
2. Product Application	● Revenue		✓	
	● Market share			✓
3. Product Delivery/ Installation	● On-time delivery	✓		
	● Customer satisfaction		✓	
	● Customer retention			✓
4. Capabilities Presentation	● Hit ratio	✓		
	● Revenue		✓	
5. Relationship Management	● Customer penetration			✓
	● Customer satisfaction		✓	
	● Customer retention			✓
	● Revenue		✓	
	● Customer profit			✓
6. Credit/Billing	● % Delinquent accounts	✓		
	● Average days outstanding		✓	
	● A/R cost			✓
7. Response to Customer Inquiries/Complaints	● Average response time	✓		
	● Customer satisfaction		✓	
	● Customer retention			✓
		Use to diagnose problems. Only reward in extreme circumstances	Use to assess contributions of key players. Screen out extraneous events	Prime territory for performance measurement

the level at which the team has the greatest influence.

Make the Final Cut

Companies must limit performance measures to the two or three that the sales team can affect most directly. □

The exercise in Exhibit 6.4 is likely to identify a number of performance measures to reward. However, companies must limit these performance measures to the two or three that the sales team can affect most directly and that will produce the most dramatic performance improvements.

Even if a measure is not rewarded monetarily, it can serve several important functions for the sales team, namely:

■ Providing an "early warning system" that indicates when sales performance may be headed off course.

■ Communicating the critical activities that make up or affect business results.

■ Testing future performance criteria (e.g., reporting customer satisfaction results prior to complete validation of a well-accepted survey methodology).

How Should You Pay for It?

Team incentives can be delivered in a number of forms that are either integrated into current compensation plans or overlayed onto existing plans as described below.

- *Incentive Pools.* An incentive pool can be funded based on a specified percentage of a business goal(s) (e.g., revenues, profits, commissions) and prespecified "shares" or percentages can be allocated to team members.

Team incentives can be delivered in a number of forms. □

- *Bonuses.* Quarterly, semiannual, or annual bonuses can be established based on a fixed percentage of salary or a fixed dollar target.

- *"Top-Hat" Program.* Using this approach, team rewards are overlayed onto existing core programs, making them easier to alter or modify without affecting existing compensation programs.

Measuring individual performance contributions to the team can be done through a "double crediting" system to encourage teamwork and diminish internal conflicts or through "split credit" systems that reflect distinct and measurable contributions to the sales process. For example, one team comprised of sales and service professionals split credit for sales 70 percent/30 percent to the sales and service rep, respectively, to reflect the level of prominence each had in the sales process.

Fitting Team Pay into the Total Rewards Equation

Team-based incentives hold an important place in a total rewards equation. □

In the end, team-based incentives hold an important place in a total rewards equation alongside base salary, commissions, and individual bonuses. To determine just how much of a place—that is, what percentage of pay—it is important to consider external factors such as competitive pay mix practices (i.e., the amount of fixed versus variable pay typical for the position and the industry), as well as internal considerations, such as the level of direct influence the team member has on performance results.

By using this four-step exercise to develop team-based incentives, companies are ensuring that they are rewarding the types of activities and behaviors that differentiate their product offerings in the marketplace, that customers value the most, and that contribute directly to the bottom line.

Companies that offer financial incentives to their employees believe in a basic tenet: One of the most effective ways to get people to do what you want them to do is to pay them for it. And in today's business world, what you pay for can be one of the greatest sources of competitive advantage.

Chapter Appendix:
Types of Team Members

There are numerous customer requirements that can be managed in a selling
team. These combinations generally fall
into three categories of team members.

One of the most effective ways to get people to do what you want them to do is to pay them for it. □

1. *Managing the Offering.* These team
    members are usually the lead contacts
    for the customer (i.e., sales reps). When
    there are multiple contacts in both the
    buying and selling organizations, they
    tend to be matched along hierarchical
    lines. For example, a national accounts
    representative would interact with the
    director of purchasing at a hospital
    chain, while sales representatives han-
    dle transactions with their contacts in
    each local hospital.

2. *Developing the Offering.* These team
    members come from different func-
    tions and do not always have direct
    contact with the customer, but still di-
    rectly influence the development of a
    product offering or bid. For example, a
    sales engineer who specs a highly tech-
    nical product may work behind the
    scenes, but his or her efforts measur-
    ably influence the outcome of that sale.

3. *Supporting the Offering.* These team members work to fulfill the actual sale once it has been closed (i.e., postsale service, reorders, etc.). Their efforts generally influence ongoing customer satisfaction. For example, if an expediter is responsible for getting the shipment to the customer within a certain time frame, his or her efforts can influence overall customer satisfaction and, consequently, the potential for subsequent customer sales.

Chapter 7

Sales Compensation in the Service Industries

By Frank X. Dowd, Principal
Alexander & Alexander Consulting Group Inc.

Introduction

The distinctions between the selling process of products and services are blurring. Service providers are trying to distinguish themselves by packaging their services into products. Conversely, you hear product producers talking of "not just pushing boxes" but providing a total service to their customers. Nevertheless, there are some lessons to be learned from several unique service sector issues. They may be of help in designing or fixing a sales compensation plan whether you sell a product or service or are making the switch.

This chapter is written to concentrate on business services—informational, financial, or supportive in nature. There are, of course, any number of services sold to the consumer. However, other marketing channels such as direct marketing or retail outlets are usually dominant. The role of professional, customer-premises sales representatives are limited at the consumer level,

The top performer in a services company will typically double the average performer's compensation. □

due to basic economics. The beginning of the chapter will discuss some unique marketing and compensation issues and practices within the services industry. Following that will be three case studies that expand on the issues and demonstrate real-world problems and solutions from actual companies. Some details of companies have been disguised to prevent identification while not diluting the sales compensation plan design issues.

Characteristics and Issues of the Service Sector

Sales professionals in the business services sector are highly paid. Market comparisons indicate a gap of 20 to 25 percent between services sector sales professionals when compared to those selling equipment, materials, or components to business customers. In addition, pay variability is much higher within a services sector company. The top earner—who is, hopefully, also the top performer—in a services company will typically double the average performer's compensation. In industrial companies, this performance premium is only 40 percent. Of course, there's more downside risk for the sales reps as well.

Making a Market

One of the reasons for the high compensation is that in some industry segments—for example, outsourced business functions— the sales rep can literally create a market where none exists. Employers today are constantly open to make/buy proposals on any number of support services. These have included, but are not limited to:

In some industry segments the sales rep can literally create a market where none exists. □

- The mailroom and supplies operations

- The entire computing center

- The human resources function

- Information systems

But there's a catch. Successful sales representatives must be professionally knowledgeable in the business being outsourced, *and* they must be accomplished enough to handle themselves all the way up to the boardroom level. In smaller companies, this selling role is often performed by top management, but in larger concerns it is a professional sales position.

This type of position is probably the most highly compensated in all the sales professions, both because of the unique requirements of an incumbent and the high potential profit impact of a successful person.

There is another selling role involved in major services programs—the account manager. □

Compensation programs are typically first-dollar commission plans, with either salaries or draws. When salaries are used, the sales professionals must typically validate their direct salaries and expenses prior to receiving commissions. Depending on the industry, commissions can range from 10 percent to 30 percent of the first year's revenues and are usually limited to new business.

Two-Step Selling Process

The reason why commissions are tied to new business or first-year business is that there is another selling role involved in such major services programs—the account manager. Many business services programs are either created or highly customized to meet the client's needs. The overall delivery process and client relationship is handled by an account manager—the second step. Most service providers have found that the skill sets needed to be effective door openers and client solution creators are different from those that are required for effective team leaders and longer-term relationship managers. Most companies are unwilling to bet their strategy on finding and keeping enough professionals who are superior in both areas. Those Renaissance people are indeed a rare breed and, therefore, well paid. It is hard enough to find, retain, and motivate the prospector/problem solvers alone. Tying up an effective executive sales professional with delivery duties has a high opportunity cost to the company and to the professional.

Tying up an effective executive sales professional with delivery duties has a high cost to the company and to the professional. □

The solution to this quandary is a team-selling environment in which both of the professionals manage the sales process by combining the best inputs of each discipline. How the duties are divided will have a lot to do with how they are paid. Several common factors usually apply, however:

■ A fixed commission pool is not split but instead either expanded pools or double payments are made to encourage team selling and cooperation. A "Win-Win" game instead of a "Zero-Sum" approach is used. Since many service provider companies are organized along client lines rather than by function, incentive design becomes critical to directing the professional's behavior. Authority, responsibility, and procedures are less well defined than in other environments.

The business services industry knows that old business is the best business. □

- We particularly favor the "first-year revenues" commission over the initial transaction. This type of plan continues to encourage the sales professional to facilitate implementation, to expand the scope of services, and to manage a smooth transition to the account manager. Nobody likes to buy something from one person and then be immediately turned over to another. This is true of someone buying an automobile or stereo, much less a million-dollar annual contract.

Relationship versus Transactional Selling

Probably the main lesson that manufacturers are learning from service companies is the value of the client relationship. The sale doesn't stop with delivery. It's just starting. Ironically, many service providers had formerly paid their account managers only on transactions—additional business. Very often there was a puritan notion of not paying for recurring business because the account manager didn't "sell" it. The business services industry knows that old business is the best business for several reasons:

- Less prospecting time and cost.

- More efficient delivery processes due to learning and adaption of the providers.

- Increased value-added services are developed over time. These can command premium prices.

- The service organization has often been designed around serving specific large accounts. A lost major client is not easily absorbed or reorganized around.

- A strong relationship can become a reference or referral—a marketing tool.

A lost major client is not easily absorbed or reorganized around. □

The compensation process for account managers has switched from the mimicking of a transaction-based process to one designed specifically for the position. Some changes are:

- More compensation weight on the "total revenues" measurement than on "new business only."

- More leverage—especially on the downside. A key function of this job is to retain the client. Compensation plans shouldn't be indifferent to a loss of part or all of the account's business. Some

New technology and changing markets have caused the explosion in the business services sector. □

first-dollar commissions or "soft-landing" bonus plans had been just that. A lost account was forgiven the account manager—i.e., "we all lost it together." True, but the account manager has the lead and, we believe, should have a personal stake in success.

■ Use of account profitability measures, where possible and in the client's best interests

■ A total business review of the account, which focuses on economic growth, quality of service, responsiveness, and client satisfaction.

Unstructured Markets

New technology and changing markets have caused the explosion in the business services sector. However, the continuing rapid change in these factors contributes to instability as well. Markets can open or close overnight. The window of opportunity for responding to market needs is quite narrow and requires flexibility in the marketing process.

For compensation plan designers, several guidelines have become clear:

■ Keep plans flexible.

- Use simple plans to shorten the learning curve for changing behaviors.

- Use a combination of several plans or components rather than one omnibus plan concept that would try to balance and include all business factors.

Perhaps the single most common design mistake is in trying to turn the incentive plan into a perfect economic model of the business. □

Perhaps the single most common design mistake is in trying to turn the incentive plan into a perfect economic model of the business. The incentive plans will become complex and difficult to adapt as the assumptions in your economic model change. Instead, isolate the one or two most important priorities for the selling job and strongly reinforce those. And, finally, as your business and markets change, don't be afraid to change your sales incentives. The critical element is knowing *when* to change. Change itself is inevitable.

The following pages contain three case studies that demonstrate these issues and suggestions.

Directory (Yellow Pages) Advertising Companies

The sales compensation practices within several companies in this industry present an interesting insight into the need for incentive designs adapting to changing market conditions and strategies.

Industry Background

The directory advertising industry experienced explosive growth during the early to mid-1980s. There were two reasons:

- The extraordinary eight-year, consumer-driven business expansion of the '80s

- The deregulation of some segments of the telecommunications industry and the breakup of the AT&T/Bell system

Since local telephone line charges remained regulated, the new regional operating companies looked to deregulated segments—like Yellow Pages—for the cash flow needed to fuel expansion and new technology. Another advantage: except for outright business failures, customer renewal rates were in the 90 percent plus area.

The Growth Years

During those high-growth years, companies took one of two approaches to paying the sales force:

- Some companies paid little or no salary; they paid first-dollar commissions on all billings, possibly with commission accelerators. As a result, some commissions skyrocketed, with top earners reaching $200,000 per year.

- Other companies paid only on net new business. This practice tended to control costs and focus the reps on growth.

In both cases, the expanding markets created a win-win situation for both the reps and the companies. Customer retention was not considered an issue due to the advertiser's need and desire to continue the listing. Since small business failures occur in any economy, disconnects were considered to be "the luck of the draw" and were often replaced in the rep's bag with some "new listings."

These "new listings" were considered to be prime selling opportunities because the sales rep was often the first media representative to call on a new business that had not yet even opened its doors to the public. In fact, new businesses could easily overbuy in this medium and have little left for local radio, newspapers, cable TV, etc.

In summary, the sales compensation plans were now revenue-driven, with less focus

Some commissions skyrocketed, with top earners reaching $200,000 per year. □

on customer satisfaction, service, or retention. And the companies received what they paid for—high growth and profits in a growth economy where the advertiser had no need to cancel.

The Transition Years

The sales compensation plans were now revenue-driven, with less regard for customer satisfaction, service, or retention. □

But nothing in business increases forever. Through the late '80s, this small business expansion slowed dramatically. As you would expect, the growth rate in advertising dipped as well. In response, companies responded both strategically and tactically.

One strategic response was to invade a neighboring company's turf with a competing directory. Some operating companies also moved from using third-party sales agencies to setting up their own sales force as a way of retaining more profits. The usual result of these strategic forays was that the telephone company would win within its own franchise area and drive out the competing directory. In some cases, the new competing directory was being sold by an experienced third-party sales force who already knew the local advertisers, while the local company's offering was sold by a newly hired, often inexperienced force. The result was the same: the local franchise would usually win out. The implications were clear:

- The nature of this service was more critical than the sales rep in influencing the sale,

- But the sales reps were being paid as if they had high selling influence.

On the compensation side, a number of companies went through a period of what might be best called denial. As sales reps' incomes fell due to the lack of growth, some companies' field sales executives lobbied for compensation plan changes geared primarily to propping up individual earnings. Among the techniques used were the following:

- Some companies increased salary levels while continuing the existing first-dollar commission plan unchanged.

- Companies that paid incentive on "net new business" would add an additional compensation component tied to renewal revenues as well.

- Other companies would calculate sales to each account separately and pay on any dollar increases to a given account. However, any account that decreased or dropped advertising would not cause a reduction in the rep's compensation.

Unfortunately, each approach was really pointed toward maintaining prior year's sales compensation levels in a declining or slowing market. Before very long, top management saw that its selling costs were increasing at a higher rate than revenues and called for change.

The Customer-Driven Years

Each approach was really pointed toward maintaining prior year's sales compensation levels in a declining or slowing market. □

The industry has now embarked on a new phase, which places emphasis on customer satisfaction and value. Compensation plan designs are following suit.

There are several organizational changes that are also being made to reflect the new market realities and an emphasis on the customer. Different companies are trying out the following approaches to assure retention of customer business:

- Several companies are segmenting their sales force along customer lines. One "natural" has been the professional market—doctors, lawyers, hospitals, consultants, accountants, and other professions. Changes in professional ethics have reduced the practitioner's historic aversion to advertising. In addition, these advertisers' needs, priorities, and sophistication are different as well. Separate, professional market sales districts are now organized in a number of companies.

- Some companies have expanded the segmentation concept to automobile agencies and other segments, with one firm having eight separate market-specific districts in each region.

- Companies have broken down the previous class distinction barrier between field reps and telesales reps by creating hybrid jobs whose choice of selling mode is in response to each customer's needs and wishes.

- Some companies have segregated "new install" sales into a separate sales team. In the past, some reps could be encouraged by the incentive plan to oversell the fledgling business owner to help offset losses at other accounts or simply to meet sales quotas. Companies found that overselling led to collection problems, cancellations, and more costly business in general.

- This industry has moved more aggressively than most into the use of telephone sales representatives aided by a

Changes in professional ethics have reduced the practitioner's historic aversion to advertising. □

Greater emphasis is being placed on overall customer satisfaction and delight. ☐

FAX machine to transmit sales presentation materials as well as prepress advertising layout proofs and price schedules. They discovered that there is less difference in whether the sales rep contacts potential customers in person or on the telephone. Service, accuracy, and responsiveness have been found to be the key factors.

On the management side, greater emphasis is being placed on overall customer satisfaction and delight. Companies have taken their TQM programs into the process of "securing and publishing customer advertising." While the actual duties of the field sales reps may or may not have been expanded, certainly their lines of sight have been extended to make them aware of longer-term customer satisfaction issues.

Compensation programs are changing in response to these changing market demands. Among some recent innovations are several initiatives:

■ A move to a higher salaries/lower incentive mix at many companies

■ More stable account assignments

■ Team incentive plans

- Customer satisfaction bonus plans

- An emphasis on total business performance

Higher Salaries. Companies had experienced difficulty in recruiting new employees due to lowered stability and credibility in their incentive opportunities. While this was an initial symptom, a more subtle effect was also occurring. The industry had long stuck to a low or no salary type of compensation mix. And while the market was expanding in all segments the concept worked well. However, as sales growth became less assured, managers would often use extra account assignments to help prop up some reps' incomes. In effect, the incentive plans became a form of "disguised salary," with more emphasis placed on sustaining reps' income levels than on paying for performance.

Stable Account Assignments. Advertising is sold once a year as annual issues are renewed. In the past, except for large accounts, an advertiser was called on once a year as part of a regional campaign or canvass. Most companies distributed account assignments with the goal of leveling earnings opportunities for all reps. As a result, most advertisers were called on by a differ-

Incentive plans became a form of "disguised salary," with more emphasis placed on sustaining reps' income levels than on paying for performance. □

In one company, the rep was actually better off financially if an account canceled completely rather than simply reduced its business. □

ent rep each year. In effect, the compensation plan—the tail—was "wagging" the entire sales campaign—the dog. This led to lowered customer satisfaction due to lack of familiarity, overselling beyond the customer's needs, errors and poor follow-up, and a lack of accountability. Next year's sales rep would lose a customer and income because of this year's rep's bad practices. As a result, the incentive plans tended to forgive reps if an account canceled and, instead, provided them with additional accounts to make up for the loss. In one company, the rep was actually better off financially if an account canceled completely rather than simply reduced its business!

Emphasis on Total Business Performance. Companies have now moved toward incentive plans that hold reps responsible for growing and maintaining the *total* business of their assigned accounts. The only forgiven loss is an outright disconnection of the telephone line—i.e., the customer is out of business. The intent is to more closely align the sales rep's income fluctuation to that of the overall business. A second key message to the sales rep is that *every customer's business is important to us.*

Customer Satisfaction Bonuses. A fortunate by-product of the regulated part of the telephone business is that most state regulators require that customer satisfaction surveys be conducted on all services, including advertising. The measurement process and a historical base is already in place. Firms have tied a significant portion of sales reps' total compensation—up to 20 percent—on measures of customer satisfaction and service. In addition, with a global satisfaction index, companies can measure quality and accuracy indicators such as:

Firms have tied a significant portion of sales reps' total compensation on measures of customer satisfaction and service. □

- Free or reduced cost space due to published errors

- Customer callbacks to correct errors

- Paperwork accuracy

- Unsigned customer orders

Another interesting measurement for incentive plan designs is the amount of business closed early in the two- to three-month canvass period. Bringing in the business at the end of a campaign causes overload and accuracy and service problems throughout the back office. Early contract closes directly contribute to customer satisfaction and, in some companies, can generate increased incentives.

Team Incentive Plans

Perhaps the most innovative program combines both organization and compensation initiatives. One company has structured an entire region along customer industry teams. Each team is dedicated to a specific industry group—medical/legal, automotive, home maintenance services, etc. While individuals' salary and targeted bonus will vary with the level of the person's duties, all team members' compensation is based on a common measurement—team results. The team includes a full spectrum of skills from major accounts managers, sales reps, and telesales reps to sales support members. The team is self-directed and weekly will allocate accounts and responsibilities as the customer needs and workloads require. Members have cooperated and assigned themselves projects such as conducting focused market research or creating sales support materials, which all members can then use. Response to the customer is no longer held captive to the schedule of one assigned rep, since the members back up and supplement each other. The initial sales results for the region—now completing its second year—are favorable when compared to other comparably sized and located regions.

Is this an early example of the future? Could be.

Information and the Business Services Industry

Background

The key theme in selling business services is the migration from transactional to relationship selling. This case study includes the approaches of three major companies providing the following services to business:

■ Long-distance services

■ Computer services and equipment

■ Local telephone services and local networks

The key theme in selling business services is the migration from transactional to relationship selling. □

What these three organizations had in common were incentive plans and selling strategies that had focused their major account managers more on individual transactions than on sustaining and growing customer relationships. In each case, the companies' markets had been entered by either new competitors, new technology, or both. Suddenly the strategic goal moved

The process of protecting current business can lead to greater penetration of the customer's total business. □

from "penetrate and grow" to "respond to the customer's needs in order to retain and protect the business." This strategy does not necessarily rule out growth. Since many business service purchasers are now consolidating their vendors into fewer but more intensive relationships, the process of protecting current business can lead to greater penetration of the customer's total business.

Each company used a sales incentive plan measurement designed to isolate the size or number of specific transactions. They based a very large part of the entire sales incentive awards on these transactional measurements. If total customer revenues or profitability were reflected in the incentive package at all, it was on a first-dollar basis, so that the component acted to provide a relatively assured amount of income to account managers with already developed accounts—"disguised salary."

Transactional Incentives

The transactional incentives used by the companies varied, but all had a common theme—"close the deal." Some examples are:

- A fixed dollar amount was paid for each line or unit of service, such as $30 per line installed.

- Specific bounties on some or all products. Often, the product marketing managers used this feature to focus the sales force on a specific item, which might well have been strategic or highly profitable but also may have been merely weak offerings. The marketers would often use these programs to steal increased "share of mind" from the rep. While marketing managers loved these plans and jockeyed for at least their "fair share," it was unclear how the company or the customer benefited.

- Many local telephone companies would estimate the first year's revenues from the sale to a business customer and pay the sales rep a lump sum commission when the deal was closed and the service started. This practice, when it was a dominant part of the compensation package, sent a clear signal—"close the deal and move on."

One difficulty that the companies experienced with transactional incentives was that they did not encourage nurturing and protecting the core business. Nor did they

Transactional incentives did not encourage nurturing and protecting the core business. □

encourage account managers to expand their contacts throughout the customer's organization. It is important to reach users who might not authorize any specific transaction, but are still very influential in defining how the overall service is being perceived. A second concern was that the account managers were not spending as much time in a consultative role aimed at expanding the customer's use of those services already being provided or in finding and correcting service delivery problems. A final and perhaps more visible difficulty was the time and effort spent by the sales force managers and staff in tracking and validating the number and details of both transactions and the commission payments.

A Move to Relationship-Driven Incentives

As companies are moving to relationship-oriented selling approaches, their compensation programs are changing as well. Several techniques are now being used in redesigning the plans for major account managers:

■ Companies have either introduced or increased the incentive amounts tied to total business revenues with the assigned account. Usually a threshold such as 80 percent of business plan is used as a qualifier for payment.

■ Other firms have redefined the slope of the pay-performance curve for the revenue-driven incentive component. Previously, this component may have been paid on a first-dollar basis. In effect, a representative at only 80 percent of plan would nevertheless receive 80 percent of his or her targeted bonus. Instead, new plans start the payment at 80 percent of plan with zero bonus. Each percentage increase above 80 percent earns 5 percent of the target incentive instead of only 1 percent. The account manager now feels a loss of business more directly.

■ Some firms will allocate a portion of the bonus program to an evaluation of the total business relationship with the customer. This review is accomplished in conjunction with the account manager's superior or a senior corporate officer assigned to act as the client advocate.

■ Other companies have tied a portion of the bonus program to customer satisfaction or quality-driven measurements.

Service users are not as likely to change a provider/client relationship unless the service is not acceptable or responsive. □

■ One company moved away from using transaction-driven incentives as "share of mind" grabbers. Instead, the transaction bonus was tied to a "customer solution" goal. A complete business review was used to identify which company services would be most useful in solving the customer's business problems. A specific incentive dollar goal was then tied to the sale of that service or product. When the selling cycle could exceed the present calendar year, a carryover was allowed. If a product or line was underrepresented in this program, it was no longer seen as the product manager being treated unfairly. Instead, it was viewed as a message from the market that that product was not viable.

The information and business services industry is one in which revenue streams can be influenced in a number of ways. Service users are not as likely to change a provider/client relationship unless the service is not acceptable or responsive. The impact of the account manager in service industries can even be more direct in preventing a loss than in acquiring expanded business. This part of the job cannot be overlooked.

Business Insurance Sales

Background

A major insurer has a separate sales organization dedicated entirely to selling retirement products in employer-sponsored programs to individuals at their workplace. In addition, the company's much larger force of sales agents may sell the same products to individuals, but in their homes. The general sales force is twenty to thirty times larger than the specialty organization and was not dispersed uniformly throughout the country.

High-front-end commissions encouraged sales representatives to prospect for new accounts rather than spend time assuring renewals or expanding policies. □

When the specialized unit was acquired by the insurer, the sales force was paid a 10 percent commission on the first year's premium and only 1 percent on renewal dollars. This arrangement meant that the insurer needed up to seven or more years of renewals before a sale would break even. (To be market competitive, margin percentages are slim and cancellation penalties can't make up the slack.) Unfortunately, these high-front-end commissions encouraged sales representatives to prospect for new accounts rather than spend time assuring the renewals or expanding the policies. Also, business with less-stable customers was encouraged by the high, front-end commission.

The field sales managers of the unit have several responsibilities:

Business with less-stable customers was encouraged by the high, front-end commission. □

- Identify and secure new employers at which their sales representatives can sell as part of the employer's overall retirement program. (Individual employees must elect to participate in the program.)

- Recruit, train, and supervise the sales force in their district.

- Act as a product line trainer and liaison with the general sales agents located within their geographic area. There could be as many as 400 to 500 agents in a single district's territory.

The district managers were paid a flat override commission of all first-year sales in their region. There was no salary nor any commission on renewals or increases. The logic was that the commission would provide the managers with incentives to prospect and secure additional employers within which their sales reps could sign on new clients.

In reality, the manager plan worked well in some parts of the country but created severe problems wherever there was a very large or aggressive general agent force in a district. The district managers' attention was distracted into maintaining liaison and training the general sales agents. Much effort also went into simply tracking transactions to assure they received proper override credits. Their new business development efforts suffered accordingly.

Incentive plans must compensate not for any sale but for a profitable sale. □

Paying for Renewals

The first change was obvious. The sales rep commission plan was changed to put equal weight on renewals and on new sales. Persistency—i.e., the renewal percentage—increased immediately. The product line became more profitable overnight. It is often the case in services that a considerable investment is made prior to sale. Not only sales expenses but also systems modifications and other startup costs can be large. The incentive plans must compensate not for any sale but for a profitable sale. Renewing an ongoing revenue stream is a key to success in many business service industries and must be rewarded. Too often, management takes a posture that the sales rep has not truly earned commissions on "old business." When there are high selling and setup costs, as in many service providers, "old business is the best business."

Defining Management Roles

The second change took more time to develop. A number of the sales managers managed districts that were strongly skewed toward the general sales agent channel. With comparable override commissions from either channel, they found it more personally profitable to spend increasing amounts of time with the general agent channel and to ignore developing business for their own subordinates. Sales representatives perceived that their own managers viewed them as merely one of several distribution channels. Unfortunately, there were two strategic problems:

Sales representatives perceived that their own managers viewed them as merely one of several distribution channels. □

1. The general sales agent channel was much stronger in the process of developing rather than in servicing a book of business. It relied more on back office support systems for customer service. Unfortunately, the retirement business is more of a high-touch service, with sales representatives usually certified as financial planners or securities dealers. Clients may get slightly better interest rates in other investments such as

mutual funds but would lose the personal service they receive.

Several years of experience have now indicated that the general agent sales force had lower persistency records, which meant too many contracts were not surviving until their break-even point. Conversely, the general agents would call on clients in their homes and were more adept at convincing individuals to roll over other retirement funds into the company's program. Since the sales managers were paid on new sales rather than on renewals, it was obvious why they preferred the general agent channel, and some were bypassing their own team.

2. The sales manager in the specialized unit *and* the sales office managers in the general agency division were both receiving front-end-loaded commissions on the same sale contract, which was more frequently canceled before the sales costs were recovered. The channel had become a double-barreled money loser.

The Management Solution

The second issue is still being resolved. In this writer's opinion, the eventual solution will require two changes: one in organization structure and the other in compensation plan design.

First, the general agent liaison role should be assigned to a newly formed group of regional coordinators with spans of control up to 1,000 agents. Training and communication would be delivered through mass media techniques. They would be paid a salary consistent with their experience as well as a more modestly targeted bonus program tied to management objectives, which included:

- Dollar volume of contracts written by general agents

- Persistency (i.e., cancellation percentage)

- Number of general agents writing above a specific dollar level per year

The new channel liaison role will bring override commissions costs down to more reasonable levels and establish role clarity for the district sales managers. The managers and their reporting representatives now comprise a team with shared goals and clear roles. The existing plan for the district managers pays the manager a commission on all new revenues generated by his or her subordinates. There is still great appeal to this plan design now that the general agent issue has been resolved. The manager's key role, after all, is to find and enroll new employers within which the sales force can sell to the company's employees. The problem was not in the commission plan design as much as in how it was being administered.

The bottom line in the services sector is that profits can be made by developing and sustaining client relationships. Sales compensation plans must be designed to focus the sales professional and the manager on one simple premise. With apologies to one apparently successful salesman, "It's the client, stupid!"

Chapter 8

Implementing a New Sales Compensation Plan

By Joanne M. Dahm, Sales Compensation Consultant
Hewitt Associates LLC

Introduction

Many organizations allocate significant resources to support
the actual creation or redesign of a sales compensation program. Unfortunately, these resources often disappear at the
most crucial time—implementation. Successfully managing all
the details of implementation can make the difference between
a new sales compensation program that works and is understood by the sales force and one that never quite lives up to its
potential.

An analogy can be made between sales compensation and
marketing. A great *product* may be slow to catch on if the
advertising, promotion, and distribution is not well executed.
A great sales compensation plan may fizzle because of inadequate transition planning, poor communication, and/or lack of
management buy-in and training.

There are three basic elements to introducing a new sales compensation program:

- Formulating a transition plan
- Communicating the new plan
- Training people on factors relevant to the new plan

First, we deal with transition planning. One approach is "to let the chips fall where they may." Another is to do it right.

Transition Planning and Strategies

Unless a sales organization is brand new, the first stage of implementation must address how to evolve from the current program to a newly designed one. A formal transition plan is not necessary if the new plan involves minor changes that can be fully effective at the start of the plan year with no special cases or considerations. However, a transition strategy is usually necessary when the mix is changing substantially or when new performance measures or standards are being used. Here are a few examples where transition plans are necessary:

1. *When the mix of base salary to incentive changes significantly.* For organizations

placing a greater portion of pay at risk, current salaries may be higher than desired. A transition strategy in this case can be either aggressive (tough), moderate, or liberal (generous to employees).

- *Aggressive.* An aggressive transition strategy reduces salaries and increases the incentive funding to immediately bring the sales force to the desired mix of pay. The downside is the apprehension that will almost surely be felt within the sales force from a reduction in the fixed portion of pay. Some organizations that are very serious about changing the culture (to a greater focus on measured, short-term performance) or making a change in the sales force profile (to one of greater risk-takers) will accept, and may even embrace, the emotion or turnover that could result from reducing base salaries. Most companies do not choose such an aggressive transition strategy, fearing counterproductive side effects.

- *Moderate.* Under a moderate transition strategy, organizations use all or some of their sales force salary increase budget to fund the incentive

A transition strategy can be either aggressive, moderate, or liberal. □

Even a moderate shift in the mix of pay will often involve freezing base salaries for several years. □

portion of the compensation plan, doing this over the period of years necessary to achieve the desired mix. Even a moderate shift in the mix of pay will often involve freezing base salaries for several years, especially in times of modest merit increase budgets. Organizations should ensure that current sales force salaries are equitable, though, before freezing the structure. Often there are certain individuals that need to have their pay brought into alignment before the current system is frozen.

Another "moderate" transition strategy calls for a gradual reduction of base salary. For example, current base salaries are maintained during the first year of the new plan, but salespeople must "earn out"[1] the difference between the new targeted base and the current base before additional incentive is earned. Everyone moves to the new base salary level and new mix of pay at the start of the second year of the new plan.

---

1 The concept of "earning out" the "excess" salary is equivalent to having a nonrecoverable draw feature in the incentive plan. That is, the difference between the current base and the lower base under the new mix becomes a draw against future incentive earnings.

This works well for a small shift in the mix of pay, e.g., from 60:40 to 50:50. For larger shifts, the reduction of salary can be done in stages.

■ *Liberal/generous.* A more liberal transition strategy is seen when companies immediately increase the incentive portion of the plan to the extent necessary to reach the desired mix, without affecting current or future base salaries. This strategy is expensive, but avoids any sales force acceptance or morale issues and it is a logical and attractive choice if total compensation levels are thought to be uncompetitive, or under market levels. Then the increased funding of the incentive plan without a corresponding base salary reduction shifts the mix of pay *and* adjusts total compensation to a desired level. In companies with competitive sales compensation levels, a liberal transition strategy is harder to justify because it can be viewed as the "easy" way out—buying the goodwill of the sales force to avoid controversy.

In companies with competitive sales compensation levels, a liberal transition strategy is harder to justify. □

2. *Another transition strategy is necessary when new performance measures or standards are uncertain or untested.* Sometimes

a sales organization decides to link pay to an uncertain performance measure—one without a historical database of results.

For example, XYZ Company chose to reward customer satisfaction, as measured by survey responses, as part of a new bonus plan. Because data had never been gathered, a standard against which to pay incentives was not established. Although a bonus scale could have been built based on predicted results, this might have resulted in over- or underpayments.

What's a good transition approach for XYZ Company? After several months, customer satisfaction survey results can be used to define a permanent standard and establish the bonus scale. In the meantime, salespeople could be paid at the "target" incentive for this portion of the incentive plan. Or, an alternative to simply paying the target incentive would be to pay people initially at one of three bonus rates based on their ranking: above average results (75th percentile and above), average results, and below average results (25th percentile or lower). As a general rule, "ranking" is not recommended in sales compensation plans because of the internal competition it fosters and the implication of designating "winners and losers" irrespective of how well or poorly the overall group performs. For temporary special circumstances (e.g., transitioning to untested performance measures), ranking can be a very helpful tool, however.

A salesperson's natural reaction might be, "Why knock myself out while they figure out what they're doing?" ☐

Running the current and new programs simultaneously for a while is another transition approach used when performance measures change drastically. This is in essence an agreement to pay out under the more favorable scenario while the new plan is "debugged," and protects the sales force against a new plan gone awry. A serious downside exists in that it provides little to no motivation for salespeople to take the new plan seriously. A salesperson's natural reaction might be, "Why knock myself out while they figure out what they're doing? I know the rules of the game on the current plan so I'll play that one as long as I can."

A preferred alternative to running the old and new compensation plans simultaneously is to provide a safety net during the transition period. This usually involves guaranteeing that "new plan" income for any individual will not drop below a certain level—for example:

■ 90 percent of last year's cash compensation

■ The average of the last two or three years' incentive compensation

■ The amount that would have been earned for achieving 95 percent of quota last year

Transition planning is only the first step to implementing a new sales compensation program. □

Transition planning is only the first step to implementing a new sales compensation program. Now it's time for "tell and sell"—communicating the program in a thorough and convincing way. Some companies are content to do communication of a new sales compensation plan in a casual way. You can be among those who choose to do it right because they don't want to do it again.

Communicating Sales Compensation

Clearly the importance of effective communication cannot be underestimated when it comes to pay programs—especially sales compensation. Why? Consider the following:

- A sales compensation plan serves as a megaphone for the strategy message. Communicating the new incentive plan, and its objectives and rationale, also reinforces the organization's business strategy. This helps focus the sales force on the objective of successfully executing the business strategy. There are few things more powerful than a highly motivated sales organization that is focused with single-mindedness on a strategy it understands and has a vested interest in executing.

  A sales compensation plan serves as a megaphone for the strategy message. □

- The sales force is almost always dispersed, with infrequent personal interaction among colleagues or with managers. A consistent and thorough communication plan becomes very important when it is a primary information source for employees.

- Some sales compensation plans require detailed explanation because they involve complicated formulas and numerous quantitative measures.

- Accustomed to sales brochures and "idea promotion," salespeople will usually have a higher expectation for attractive, marketing-oriented communication. They expect the company to "sell" the new plan, spelling out the features and benefits in an unambiguous way. This signals the importance of the changes to the company.

Turnover is often higher in the sales force than elsewhere in the organization. □

■ The sales force typically has a relatively good knowledge of competitive pay plans and practices, or at least they have anecdotal insights gained through conversation with peers and recruiters. Therefore, thoughtful communication about the competitive positioning of the new plan may be needed to assure participants that the company was aware of these reference points.

■ Turnover is often higher in the sales force than elsewhere in the organization, which means that a sales compensation plan may have to be explained more or less continuously throughout the plan year for new sales employees. Effective communication materials and effectively trained line managers who can communicate the plan become even more important when turnover is high.

Tips on strategies for communicating sales compensation programs include:

■ *Communication should be planned and continuous.* When communicating about a complicated, sensitive, and perhaps emotional topic the material is easier to understand if presented in small, manageable pieces or if repeated often. Even if the incentive program doesn't change, ongoing issues are sure to arise that will need to be communicated. When a sales compensation change is extensive or could be perceived as a "takeaway," or if it is likely to elicit a strong emotional response, stage-setting communication is essential. Preliminary discussion of the plan change and sales compensation philosophy with line managers, or even with opinion leaders within the sales force, can make or break the broad-based acceptance of the plan. This type of advance communication can be informal, but still must be well planned, thorough, and used as a learning exercise for the eventual plan communication.

Even if the incentive program doesn't change, ongoing issues are sure to arise. □

■ *Communication should focus on the "why" as well as the "what."* Employees need to understand the underlying purpose of the compensation program, as well as the details of how it works. If salespeople accept your objectives for changing the plan, they are more likely to accept the new plan.

If salespeople accept your objectives for changing the plan, they are more likely to accept the new plan. □

■ *Open communication works best.* A straightforward discussion of what the plan will and won't do, as well as what it is intended to do, will help build trust among the sales force. One truism in sales compensation is that people will figure out what the plan will and won't do anyway, so it is better to discuss these points up front. For example, consider a company moving to an increased emphasis on pay-for-performance. It is much more effective to present the plan as paying less to those below quota and more to those above quota than to present a new commission schedule and let the sales force figure out the impact on their own.

■ *Communicate the effect of the compensation plan change, preferably on an individual basis.* Some salespeople are subjected to frequent compensation plan changes. Because continual changes to the compensation rules can produce feelings of "salesperson abuse," it becomes very important to tell people clearly how the change will affect them. Otherwise there is a natural impression that "they like to keep us off balance by changing the compensation plan just when I am getting it figured out and starting to do well under it."

The preferred method would be to show each individual, via a printed worksheet, electronic spreadsheet, or personal explanation, how their past performance would pay out under the new plan and what they would have to do to increase their earnings under the new plan. If individualized worksheets are problematic, you can present several hypothetical performance scenarios that highlight the effect of the new plan on earnings.

The preferred method would be to show each individual how their past performance would pay out under the new plan. □

- *Use a variety of media to communicate the plan.* There is no one best way to communicate compensation plan changes. Different individuals absorb information best from various media. Often a combination of meetings, print, video, and personalized statements should be used. Audience size, geography, available preparation time, and budget are all considerations. Regardless, one-on-one communication with each individual's manager is essential to an effective communication process.

Generally, bringing salespeople together for a new plan rollout, even if only by district or office, is a preferred communication format. This ensures that people receive a consistent message and that adequate time is taken to explain the new plan and philosophy. It also provides a forum for people to ask questions, receive consistent answers, and to discuss the changes among themselves, which can increase acceptance by increasing understanding.

A national sales meeting provides a forum for establishing an overriding and consistent theme, but it is not always an option due to cost and time constraints. Furthermore, a national meeting announcement without follow-up district or regional meetings will diminish the active participation of line managers. Sales managers will almost always be the key messengers of a sales compensation change. A national sales meeting announcement is never a sufficient substitute for their direct involvement in the communication process.

Written materials such as brochures, overheads, question and answer guides, etc., can be helpful to augment the messages introduced in meetings. A videotape that communicates the strategy behind the plan as well as plan basics can be very effective as an introduction to a more detailed explanation.

Sales managers will almost always be the key messengers of a sales compensation change. □

Training

The last element of implementing a new compensation plan is training. "Training" is viewed as an expendable and expensive overhead item in many organizations. However, there is a large group of companies that place a high value on training— these companies have a different opinion.

The last element of implementing a new compensation plan is training. □

Training related to a new sales compensation plan can take several tracks:

- Training managers on how to communicate the new plan philosophy and mechanics to their salespeople

- Training managers on elements of administering the plan in the field

- Training salespeople about what they need to accomplish to "win" under the sales compensation plan

- Training salespeople on how to adopt new behaviors and techniques

Training managers is necessary for a "cascade" communication strategy, where line managers are given all of the tools and information needed to roll out a new plan in the field. A successful strategy presents the same materials to managers that they will introduce to their salespeople but also includes training sessions in which managers can role-play, anticipate questions and answers from salespeople, or practice their own presentation.

Including objectives in the sales bonus plan heightened people's concerns about fairness and consistency. □

A second training focus can spotlight an element of the new compensation plan for which managers are responsible. For example, let's examine a company that implements individualized performance objectives as a critical part of the bonus determination. Although evaluations had been a feature of the company's merit increase process, including objectives in the sales bonus plan heightened people's concerns about fairness and consistency across the field organization. District managers were brought together for an explanation of the elements of the evaluation, definitions of performance factors, and examples of different levels of performance. Most importantly, they participated in group exercises where they rated several fictional salespeople based on qualitative and quantitative descriptions of their performance. They then discussed the ratings and their rationale for assigning them with other managers. Management confidence and skills were built, as was field support for the new program.

Training might also be targeted toward a very technical part of the compensation plan which managers must understand. For example, if the company is moving to a territory profit contribution measure, sales managers might receive training on how to read and interpret the financial statements, and learn how to most effectively impact profit measures at a district or regional level.

Finally, training might focus on behavior changes needed by salespeople to be successful under the new compensation plan. This type of training is especially important, and usually only necessary, when the new compensation plan is shifting performance measures to something previously underemphasized. The company mentioned earlier as implementing a customer satisfaction measure also implemented a training program on how to service its customers most effectively. Another company decided to have field financial managers hold sessions in each region to train salespeople on their impact on regional profits, after the company shifted from a volume to a profit measure.

The three key areas—transitioning, communicating, and training—are critical to ensuring a successful sales compensation plan rollout. Take the time to do it right. Too many good sales compensation plans are abandoned because they are not given a chance to succeed. In the words of one sales executive in the midst of planning a sales compensation change:

Too many good sales compensation plans are abandoned because they are not given a chance to succeed. □

"*This* time, we are allocating as much time and effort to the implementation of our new sales compensation plan as to the plan design project. Last time, we seriously underestimated the planning, communicating, and execution of the transition from 'old' to 'new.' We paid a very steep price in terms of confusion, confidence in our management team, and even diminished sales productivity. It won't happen again!"

Chapter 9

Recruiting and Developing Salespeople: The Power of Sales Compensation

By Bill O'Connell, Principal
and Lisa Bush Hankin, Senior Consultant
Sibson & Company

Introduction

Current conventional wisdom has finally caught on to what sales and marketing managers have known all along—good salespeople are extremely hard and expensive to find. So when they find the right salespeople, managers want to do everything possible to make salespeople both successful and eager to stay with the company.

As part of the recruitment and retention/development processes, no time is more critical than the first two years. On the one hand, new salespeople need training and support to make it over the learning curve to become fully productive and successful. At the same time, however, the more productive they become, the more vulnerable these salespeople are to turnover. To help salespeople through these critical years, companies have a number of tools, such as sales compensation, training, performance reviews, coaching, and mentoring, that can be used as parts of an overall effort to recruit and retain sales talent. (See Exhibit 9.1.)

This chapter will focus on how sales compensation can be used in the recruiting process by providing the conceptual model for analyzing a company's specific sales recruiting challenges, a description of sales compensation techniques that can be used in the context of recruiting and developing salespeople, and a framework for determining when and how to use these sales compensation techniques in the recruitment/development process.

How Do You Pay New Recruits?

When it comes to thinking about how to pay new sales recruits, many companies' first reaction is simply to put new salespeople on the regular sales incentive program. Unfortunately, this approach ignores the fact that most sales incentive plans have little value as a retention tool

Exhibit 9.1   Making the Development Process Easier

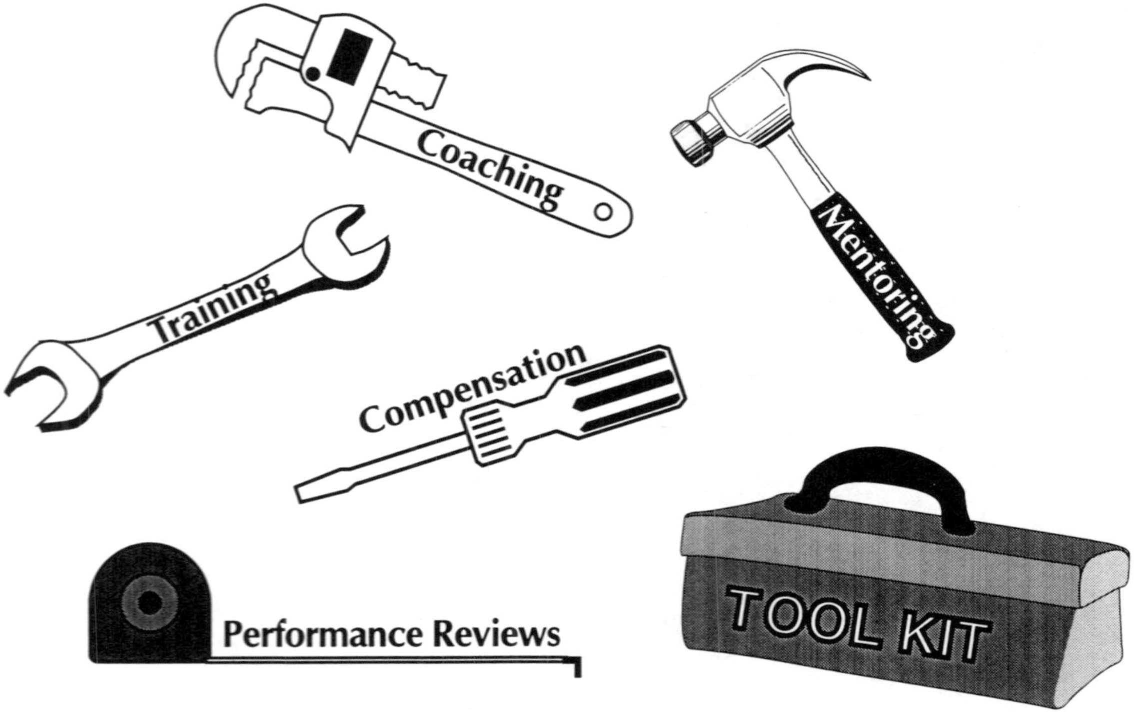

Mentoring

Coaching

Training

Compensation

Performance Reviews

TOOL KIT

Source: Sibson & Company

Even new salespeople who have experience at other organizations must get over the learning curve in their new position. □

because new sales reps are not yet fully productive and stand to make little money under the plan. So a logical alternative may be to develop an interim or bridge sales compensation plan for new recruits during their initial tenure with the company.

When deciding whether an interim plan is worth the extra cost and effort and what kind of program would be most effective, it is helpful to consider four major concepts—the learning curve, the company's cost of turnover, employee susceptibility to turnover, and the company's ability to attract candidates. (See Exhibit 9.2.)

Learning Curve

Much has been written about the length of time it takes for new salespeople to "get up to speed" and become productive. Even new salespeople who have experience at other organizations must get over this learning curve in their new position. How long does this usually take? It depends. Each organization has its own unwritten assumptions about the length of time it takes for a new salesperson to make it over the learning curve to reach full productivity.

In the learning curve in Exhibit 9.3, Area A represents the period right after a new·

Exhibit 9.2   Do You Need a Bridge Compensation Arrangement?

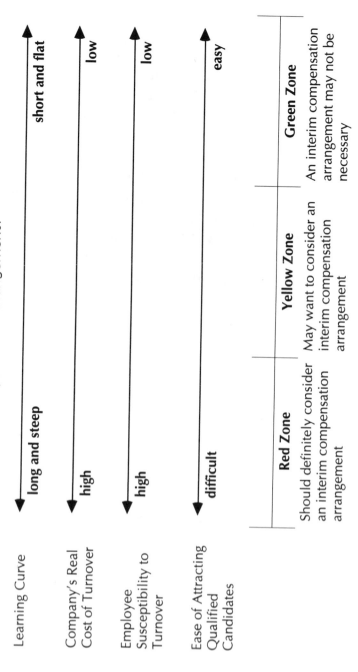

Source: Sibson & Company

salesperson is hired. At this time, as the salesperson starts learning rapidly about the company, its products, its customers, and its competitors, productivity increases markedly. However, most of this knowledge has not yet been "field tested" in a selling situation. In Area B, learning continues as the new salesperson tests this knowledge in actual selling situations. During this stage, the new salesperson gains a firm grasp of the basics and has opportunities to use them in the field. The salesperson initiates contacts with accounts and begins to prioritize them and move them through the selling process. In Area C, a salesperson experiences an entire sales cycle and increases in productivity gradually begin to slow. During this stage, the salesperson operationalizes learnings and becomes familiar with the physical geography and efficiencies of the assigned territory, as well as with the various contacts, influencers, decision makers, and champions within customer organizations. Eventually, in Area D, the new salesperson integrates these learnings and begins to form enduring bonds with customers as productivity gradually reaches 100 percent.

Every company's sales learning curve takes a different shape, with the length and

Exhibit 9.3

Illustrative "Learning Curve" for New Salespeople

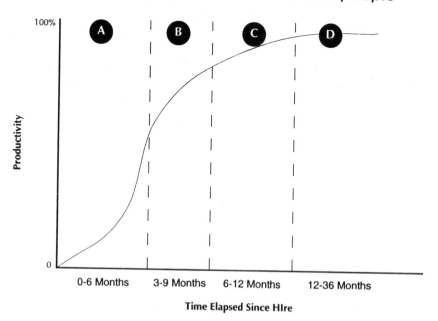

Area	Approximate Time Frame*	Activities
A	0–6 months	• Learning about company, products, customers, competitors
B	3–9 months	• Using "the basics" in field selling situations
		• Learning accounts, contacts
C	6–12 months	• Experiencing an entire sales cycle
		• Learning territory geography, efficiencies, prioritization
D	12–36 months	• Developing lasting bonds with customers
		• Integrating all learnings

* Actual length of time will vary by each company's situation

Every company's sales learning curve takes a different shape. □

steepness of the curve affected by factors such as product line complexity, length of the selling cycle, competitiveness of the marketplace, and complexity of territory/customer base. A company can actually determine the shape of its learning curve for new salespeople by charting the historical productivity—as measured by revenues, quota achievement, volume, margins, etc.—of all incumbents during the first six months on the job, second six months on the job, and so on.

When it comes to using the learning curve as a basis for compensation treatment, companies usually employ one of two philosophies. One company may find its learning curve is short enough to preclude the need for any special compensation arrangements to tide new sales reps over until they reach a productive level. In fact, these companies may view the resulting financial hardship as making sales reps hungrier. Another company may realize that it takes significant time for new salespeople to get up to speed and recognize the need for a compensation "bridge" to help sales reps get by financially until they become productive enough to sustain themselves. Companies that operate under this latter philosophy usually do not bridge the rep to full productivity, but to some point less than that. For these companies the question is, how long is long enough and how long is too long?

Cost of Turnover

The decision regarding whether and how to bridge new reps' compensation is often determined by a company's cost of turnover. The more expensive it is for the company to lose a new salesperson, the more likely it is that the company will or should provide some sort of compensation bridge for new salespeople. The cost component factors that drive the cost of turnover can be separated into "hard" costs—actual dollars that can be tracked—and "soft" costs—costs that have a real and sometimes greater financial impact on the company, but cannot be directly tracked. (See Exhibit 9.4.)

The more expensive it is for the company to lose a new salesperson, the more likely it is that the company will provide some sort of compensation bridge for new salespeople. □

These hard or measurable costs of turnover are determined by the recruiting and training investment made in new reps and the cost of business lost because of sales rep turnover.

1. *Recruiting costs.* The costs of finding new sales reps—including advertisements, recruitment firm fees, and management time spent reviewing resumes and interviewing, evaluating, and se-

Exhibit 9.4   The Cost of Turnover

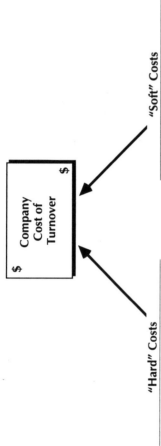

"Hard" Costs

- Recruiting expenses
  - Advertising
  - Placement Fees
  - Management Time
    - Interviewing
    - Evaluation
    - Selection
- Training expenses
- Cost of lost business due to territory vacancy

Company Cost of Turnover

"Soft" Costs

- Customer "bad will"
- Damage to company reputation
- Decline in employee morale
- Lost customer relationships
- Loss of proprietary information

Source: Sibson & Company

lecting candidates—factor into the decision of whether and how to bridge new rep compensation. In general, a company is more likely to use an interim compensation plan if the cost of finding candidates is higher than the additional cost of the interim plan.

Recruiting costs are primarily influenced by the skill set required of new sales reps. Although many companies do not formally define and articulate the skills and attributes that make a successful new hire, they still have a good idea of what it takes to become a successful salesperson. For example, if a high-technology company's most successful salespeople have three to five years of engineering work experience, knowledge of high-end computer equipment, and a marketing degree, that company's recruiting costs are likely to be higher than those of a consumer products company that primarily hires college graduates with no previous full-time work experience. The rarer the skill set, the higher the costs will be for recruiting or replacing a sales rep.

2. *Training costs.* By the same token, the higher its investment in training new

Recruiting costs are primarily influenced by the skill set required of new sales reps. □

The higher the cost of business lost due to territory vacancy, the higher the cost of turnover to the company. □

salespeople, the higher a company's cost of turnover will be. Although training investment makes reps productive faster and reduces the likelihood that they will leave because of frustration, it also makes them *more* attractive to competitors. For example, for years, the Xerox training program was extremely successful in helping Xerox to build a world-class selling organization. But the program also unintentionally provided its competitors and other sales organizations with a steady stream of well-trained Xerox salespeople.

3. *Cost of lost business.* The cost of business lost because of unstaffed sales territories and unassigned accounts is another major hard cost of turnover. While it is difficult to be precise, most companies have at least some idea of how much revenues decrease when a territory is unassigned. The higher the cost of business lost due to territory vacancy, the higher the cost of turnover to the company.

The soft costs of turnover, while nearly impossible to quantify, increase the magnitude of the hard costs. These soft costs include customer "bad will" created by frequent personnel shifts that change the face in front of the customer and disrupt accounts; damage to the company's reputation caused by disgruntled ex-employees and irate customers; low employee morale; customer relationships and their associated revenue potential that partially or completely leave the company with the departed salesperson; and loss of proprietary information, such as training materials and account information (not to mention the secret formula for the company's product!), that the departed employee takes to another, possibly competing organization. All these costs must be considered when calculating the overall cost of turnover to the company.

Employee Susceptibility to Turnover

In general, the more likely a sales rep is to leave the company, the more the company might want to consider a bridge compensation arrangement. Two of the major influences on turnover from the reps' viewpoint are their perceived return on time (PROT) and the number and nature of other career opportunities.

Individuals starting out as salespeople do so in large part because of the financial

The risk of turnover increases when salespeople have other, more attractive employment opportunities. □

return on the time spent in the new position. If salespeople believe that there will be a favorable financial return from their association with the company, they are more likely to stay in that position. If the financial return appears to be smaller than expected, or too far in the future, the salesperson may be inclined to explore opportunities with other companies.

Some of the factors influencing a salesperson's PROT include the income-producing potential of the person's assigned territory; the nature and number of leads; the viability of the product or service to be sold at the going price; advertising and other marketing support; training and other sales support; and the length and steepness of the learning curve. Without being too generous or too stingy, bridge compensation arrangements can help reps perceive a reasonable return on time and make them more comfortable while they wait for a payoff from their sales efforts.

At the same time, the risk of turnover increases when salespeople have other, more attractive employment opportunities. Companies in industries that commonly raid competitors' sales talent generally provide a greater number of career opportunities for sales reps. This situation is most likely to occur in industries, like computer software, that are growing quickly and where the demand for qualified sales candidates exceeds the available supply. In addition, some industries and companies are seen as training grounds for qualified salespeople. Companies that offer superior training and development of new employees—IBM and Xerox are good examples—are more susceptible to losing new *and* experienced salespeople.

Some industries and companies are seen as training grounds for qualified salespeople. □

Attractiveness to Candidates

If a company does not provide at least a minimal income to new salespeople, candidates may turn down the company's employment offers solely for that reason. Bridge compensation arrangements can help overcome this negative in the recruiting process, enabling companies to hire those high-potential candidates with personal financial commitments, like a home mortgage, who would likely go elsewhere.

Attracting candidates also depends on how well the sales compensation is communicated—even if a bridge arrangement doesn't exist—during the recruiting process. Search firms indicate that candidates for sales positions are much more likely

Experienced sales candidates abhor artificial caps on incentive opportunities. □

than candidates for other types of positions to ask about compensation early on in the recruiting process. Not only are candidates concerned about the earning opportunity and the structure of the sales compensation plan (especially performance measures and timing of payouts), but they also demand to know exactly how incentive earnings are calculated. Not surprisingly, experienced sales candidates abhor artificial caps on incentive opportunities and are generally unwilling to move to a new company without a first-year guarantee that is at least equal to their most recent full year's earnings, or to their annualized current year earnings.

To market a company's sales compensation plan to candidates, John Doyle of the search firm Paul Ray Berndtson suggests that companies make sure the plan is understandable both in terms of its structure and in how the individual salesperson can control earning levels. Companies should also emphasize the short-term components of the plan over the longer-term components, such as insurance policy trailers and ongoing renewal bonuses. Candidates tend to discount long-term earnings potential and focus on what can be earned in the short term (one year or less). And finally, companies should keep the sales compensation program in perspective. A good compensation program alone generally will not help land a "hot" candidate. But a badly designed or poorly communicated program can definitely act as a barrier, even when all the other aspects of the job are desirable.

The best sales managers approach their job as if recruiting doesn't end until the employee has been on the job six months. Accordingly, a company needs to sell its compensation plan to new salespeople both before and after they're hired. The key is to make the plan understandable to an outsider, using quantitative examples; emphasize the earnings opportunity, not the plan's structure; provide the new rep with frequent tracking of performance that can easily be translated into potential earnings; and never lie or set false expectations. And finally, a bridge arrangement is likely to increase the attractiveness of even a well-explained plan.

A company needs to sell its compensation plan to new salespeople both before and after they're hired. □

Techniques

If all these considerations point to the need for an interim or bridge compensation arrangement, a company can utilize or combine various techniques, including base salary, recoverable and nonrecoverable draws, guarantees, mentor-based team selling, milestone-based incentives, and managers' compensation.

Base Salary

One of the simplest ways to ease the transition period for new salespeople is to pay them a straight base salary for a given period of time. Using base salary as a bridge for new salespeople is appropriate when:

- It is difficult to measure the salesperson's contribution accurately.
- The job requires a significant amount of nonselling work.
- The company uses team selling extensively.
- The salesperson is unlikely to close any unassisted sales in the short term.
- The company reassigns territories, accounts, and salespeople frequently.
- The sales job requires significant knowledge and experience that would draw a base salary elsewhere—for example, engineering expertise.

If several of these conditions apply to new salespeople, paying a straight base salary may be appropriate. On the flip side, paying base salary can be less motivating by reducing the salesperson's financial "hunger," while increasing the company's fixed costs. It may also be demotivating to new salespeople who make many early sales but receive no incentives.

Draws

For those companies that don't want to pay a base salary to new reps, using recoverable or nonrecoverable draws may be a more attractive option.

A recoverable draw is essentially an advance against expected future incentive earnings that the salesperson pays back to the company from incentive earnings once he or she starts to earn incentive pay. Accordingly, a recoverable draw provides the same kind of financial safety net to the new salesperson as a personal bank loan. As such, recoverable draws provide financial stability to the employee but are less costly to the company and, arguably, motivate the new salesperson to start earning incentive pay.

However, recoverable draws create paperwork and its associated administrative expense and don't really provide any of the other advantages of base salary besides financial stability.

Paying base salary can be less motivating by reducing the salesperson's financial "hunger." □

Sales reps may hesitate to draw as much as they need to live on when they first start with the company. □

With nonrecoverable draws, the individual does not have to pay the company back, making it essentially a flexible base salary that the salesperson receives on an as-needed basis. Nonrecoverable draws also create less paperwork. However, sales reps may hesitate to draw as much as they need to live on when they first start with the company, thereby reducing the nonrecoverable draw's retention value. Or knowing it doesn't have to be paid back, sales reps may abuse the draw, for example, by taking time to search for another job. In the latter case, the company might consider setting a limit on nonrecoverable draws while allowing higher amounts to be drawn on a recoverable basis.

Guarantees

Guarantees are a commitment that a new salesperson *will not earn less than* a fixed amount over a given amount of time with the company, although they may indeed earn more. Under these arrangements, if the salesperson earns less than the guarantee amount, the company makes up the difference. This arrangement provides the salesperson with assurance that the company's "money is where its mouth is" when it assigns a new salesperson to a territory that the company says is viable.

However, the guarantee generally is not paid if the rep leaves the company before the end of the guarantee period. In addition, guarantees create minimal paperwork. However, they don't provide the rep with financial stability in the critical early period with the company, unless a base salary is also being paid, because the salesperson is not likely to be earning much incentive pay early on. For this reason, it makes the most sense to use guarantees if the sales compensation plan has both base salary and incentive components.

Milestone-Based Incentives

Another alternative is to put new reps on an interim incentive plan tied to certain objectives and milestones in the sales development process. For example, a sales rep may receive an incentive payout for satisfactory completion of various training programs or modules; assisting an experienced rep in closing a sale; achieving product or industry knowledge milestones; completing a developmental rotation to another department, such as customer service; the number of presentations made; introducing a sales specialist into the account; or booked but not yet collected sales.

Team Selling

Another way of easing new sales reps' development and increasing their earning potential is to team them with an experienced salesperson for a period of time. This provides training and mentoring to the new rep and better service to customers. The compensation arrangements for this team can be structured in a number of ways, which are ranked from most to least costly:

1. Pay full commission to both the new and the experienced reps for all sales.

2. Pay the experienced rep full commission to encourage the experienced rep to take on a trainee, while the new rep receives a partial commission for all sales.

3. Split commissions between the new and experienced reps, although this is not recommended because it creates a disincentive for the experienced rep to introduce the new rep to promising situations.

Of course, the company also has the option of paying new reps a base salary with no incentive for the time they are teamed up with the experienced rep.

Managerial Compensation Arrangements

A discussion of sales compensation for new salespeople is not complete without a mention of the compensation arrangements for their managers. Probably the most common method of compensating sales managers is paying them an override on the earnings of the sales reps they manage. While this seems to provide incentives for managers to have their new sales reps succeed, a straight override can actually encourage managers to keep adding reps to a territory until the marginal revenue brought in by the last rep is zero. In other words, under a straight override, it is in the manager's interest to keep adding reps as long as each one is bringing in *something*—no matter how small—so that the manager can earn an override. But if a sales rep's territory isn't large enough to make a living, that rep will leave the company.

The most common method of compensating sales managers is paying them an override on the earnings of the sales reps they manage. □

There are a number of alternatives to paying managers a straight override. The following two alternatives make the most sense from the standpoint of recruiting and developing new salespeople:

1. Reward sales managers on the overall profitability of the territories they man-

age by including in the calculation of profitability all hiring, turnover, and indirect employee costs, such as benefits; or

A straight override can actually encourage managers to keep adding reps to a territory until the marginal revenue brought in by the last rep is zero. □

2. Reward sales managers on the attainment of strategic milestones tied to the success of new reps in their territories—for example, paying managers a bonus based on the number of reps who exceed a threshold level (set so that a rep can make a satisfactory living) of production and paying a bonus based on the percent of their direct reps who achieve a threshold level of sales. For example, managers may have an opportunity to earn 10 percent of annual base salary if 50 percent of their reps reach 100 percent of quota, 20 percent of base salary if 70 percent of their reps reach 100 percent of quota, and 40 percent of base salary if 90 percent of their reps reach 100 percent of quota.

When and How to Use These Tools

When recruiting salespeople, compensation can be a double-edged sword. In trying to make a sales compensation plan "user-friendly" to new employees, companies can go too far, only to end up with a group of happy laggards instead of productive salespeople. On the other hand, a company that is a little tougher with its money can build a revolving door of new salespeople who burn bridges with the company's customers as they go.

When recruiting salespeople, compensation can be a double-edged sword. □

The basic way to address this compensation challenge is to determine the incremental compensation cost the company is willing to pay to avoid the costs of turnover and to bring new reps up to full productivity using the following steps:

1. *Calculate the hard and soft costs of turnover per employee.* This is a very slippery number, but it is the magnitude, not the precision, of the costs that is important.

2. *Analyze past turnover data[1] to gain an understanding of when new salesperson turnover is most likely to occur.* This will provide insight into whether there are any "critical points" in the development of new reps when they are most likely to leave. This will indicate when and for how long any bridge compensation arrangement should be in place.

---

1 In normal circumstances it would be useful to distinguish desired turnover (e.g., reps who managers believed "weren't cutting it") from undesired turnover (reps that the company was sorry to see go). However, with new salespeople who leave in the developmental period it is often too difficult to distinguish these.

3. *Determine the approximate length and steepness of the new salesperson learning curve.* This will give further insight into how long to extend any interim compensation arrangements.

4. *Interview a sample of ex-employees* to determine what factors contributed to their decisions to leave the company. This should give some qualitative insight into the nature of the problem.

Armed with these facts, the company can decide whether interim compensation arrangements are in fact necessary. For example, if a company's sales learning curve is relatively short and not very steep, or if turnover hasn't been a problem, interim compensation arrangements may be unnecessary. However, if the company determines that it does indeed require some sort of interim compensation program, it must decide how much it is willing to spend on such measures. This number can be zeroed in on by using the company's cost of turnover as the *maximum* allocation and then determining what amount below that the company is willing to invest to reduce turnover and attract new employees. And finally, the company must determine what form this compensation program should take—for example, will the company rely on base salary, draws, or some other approach?—and how long it should be in place. Based on the length of the learning curve, the critical points for turnover, and the incremental compensation costs it is willing to incur, a company can figure out how long it can afford to provide bridge compensation to new salespeople.

For most companies, the decision of whether to provide a bridge compensation arrangement comes down to a simple question: "Can we afford not to?"

The decision of whether to provide a bridge compensation arrangement comes down to a simple question: "Can we afford not to?" ☐

Chapter 10

Paying the Sales Manager

By John K. Moynahan, Consultant
William M. Mercer, Incorporated

Introduction

The first-level sales manager plays a pivotal role in accomplishing a company's marketing objectives. The manager must be a coach and advisor to the sales force, while at the same time retaining a management perspective. The sales manager must supervise and motivate a group of individuals who may frequently earn more than the manager. It is often said that being "promoted" from sales representative to sales manager involves an opportunity to work harder and be paid less. How, then, should a company reward the sales manager position in a manner consistent with the incentives offered both field sales and other managers?

The answer, as it is to so many compensation issues, is "it depends." Each situation must be considered in the unique context of an organization. In the remainder of this chapter, we examine the factors to consider in designing the sales management incentive compensation program. General considerations influencing the size and nature of sales management incentive opportunity include:

It is unlikely that the field sales manager would participate in a senior executive bonus plan. □

■ *The size of the manager's incentive opportunity relative to the range of opportunities available to field sales subordinates as well as to the competitive labor market for sales managerial talent.* This is not to suggest that the compensation structure should eliminate overlap in the pay of representatives and managers, but a company is wise to avoid a situation in which sales representatives (other than the most exceptional ones) routinely outearn the sales manager.

■ *Overall organizational climate, culture, or personality.* The program selected for compensating the sales manager must fit comfortably into the value system of the organization.

■ *Compatibility with the compensation program offered to peer executives in nonsales functions.* For example, if participation in the senior executive bonus plan is extended downward to peers of the field sales manager, then field sales managers should probably participate in the plan. It is unlikely, however, that the field sales manager would participate in a senior executive bonus plan with restricted eligibility; rather, an incentive plan for sales managers only should be developed.

■ *The career path associated with a sales manager position.* If the managerial position is one that is occupied by a career manager who may move into senior management, the incentive opportunity while in sales management should not be so lucrative as to discourage further career advancement.

While the aforementioned issues are important in determining the potential range of the sales manager's pay, the key concept indicating the proper *design* of sales manager compensation is the prominence of the sales force supervised.

The key concept indicating the proper design of sales manager compensation is the prominence of the sales force supervised. □

Types of Sales Managers

It is possible to categorize sales managers by whether the prominence of the sales force is high or not. Table 10.1 illustrates the different characteristics of the two categories of sales force, and the resultant differences in the role of the field sales manager.

The appropriate approach to sales manager compensation becomes apparent as it

follows the results for which they are accountable:

Average Productivity =
   Objectives Based Bonus
   e.g., Volume (Performance to Quota) and/or
   Nonvolume (Key Account Goals, New Account Goals, etc.)

Aggregate Productivity =
   "Override"
   (Percentage of Subordinates' Commissions)

Table 10.1

Contrasting Types of Sales Forces

Low/Medium Prominence	High Prominence
High Fixed Costs	Low Recruiting, Training Costs
Accounts Owned by Company	Accounts Owned by Sales Representatives
Accounts Can Be Reassigned	Sales Representatives Not Interchangeable
Salary or Salary + Bonus	Commission Pay Plan
Role of Manager: Define Tactics Which if Executed Will Improve <u>Average</u> Productivity	Role of Manager: Recruit, Retain, Motivate to Higher <u>Individual</u> Productivity

Industrial Managers

Looking first at the typical industrial sales manager, we observe that this manager is responsible for:

- A relatively fixed resource (number of territories)

- An organizational structure, including size of staff, that is generally determined by a higher level of management

- Sales representatives who are comparatively expensive to recruit, train, and replace

- A sales force that must service and sell to an assigned group of accounts that are loyal to the company rather than to the individual representative

- Business volume that is affected by both internal (sales effectiveness) and external (economic) factors in any account, territory, or time period

Given these job characteristics, the most logical compensation approach is a *"results-oriented" bonus*. Here, the manager earns a bonus that is tied to success in meeting a predetermined range of results, usually expressed in terms of the aggregate volume of the territories supervised.

The sales manager's success depends entirely on subordinates' efforts. □

If sales fall short of these results, no bonus is earned; if sales surpass set levels by a wide margin, maximum bonus is earned. If sales match expected levels, bonus, in combination with base salary, will bring total cash compensation up to targeted competitive levels.

In general, the same principles apply to incentive compensation designed for sales representatives and sales managers: (1) use of a method that encourages both employer and participants to maximize earnings, and (2) selection of goals that communicate and reinforce the important activities and results expected from the participant. With respect to the industrial field sales manager, however, there are two complicating factors:

1. Unlike the sales representative, whose bonus depends on personal efforts, the sales manager's success depends entirely on subordinates' efforts. Therefore, the field sales compensation plan must motivate the manager to deploy staff in the most effective way and to communicate and reinforce goals that will, collectively, yield the sales volume targeted for the entire district or region.

2. As the manager moves up in an organization, compensation opportunities

will be increasingly affected by uncontrollable circumstances. (For example, the aggregate value of the chief executive's compensation package generally depends heavily on stock market activity, a factor over which the CEO has virtually no control.)

Therefore, while the basic principles of compensation design for managers and representatives are similar, the differences in their roles should be addressed in the design of the plan. Because managers face increasing compensation risks as they move up the organizational ladder, and because fluctuations in territorial volume are likely to be less severe when aggregated at a district or regional level, the sales manager compensation plan can generally be more strongly linked to volume than would be appropriate for a field sales representative. A manager, can, after all, alleviate any shortfalls in volume in one geographic territory or specific industry by deploying resources more effectively elsewhere.

In view of these distinctive characteristics, the results-oriented bonus generally is the appropriate approach for the industrial sales manager. This method produces a system of checks and balances that (1) enables the manager, through the use of field

As the manager moves up in an organization, compensation opportunities will be increasingly affected by uncontrollable circumstances. □

sales compensation plans, to deploy resources in a way that should produce the results for which the manager is held accountable (usually district-wide volume and/or profit) and (2) reflects the manager's skill in setting and communicating goals that, if met, will actually produce the desired volume results.

If management's goals are too demanding, the volume results may be achieved, but sales representatives will be dissatisfied. ☐

If management's goals are too demanding, the volume results may be achieved, but sales representatives will be dissatisfied because they will not have reached their goals; but if goals are too easy or inappropriate, even though the sales representatives may earn an award, the manager's own earnings will suffer. In effect, through the results-oriented method, the manager is challenged to improve the company's return (sales volume) on a fixed investment (a number of territories with a fixed number of selling hours to be utilized), thereby effectively improving the *average* productivity of subordinates. To achieve this end, the manager must have a say in establishing both the volume and nonvolume goals that will be communicated to the field sales force and incorporated in the field sales incentive compensation plan.

Through the results-oriented bonus, the manager has greater incentive to create a link between the company's goals and sales representatives' goals. By establishing, rather than simply monitoring, the relevant, achievable objectives that will yield the desired aggregate results, the manager will improve sales force productivity, and earn a larger bonus.

Entrepreneurial Sales Force Managers

Next, consider the appropriate sales management incentive strategy for the manager of an "entrepreneurial" sales force, such as life insurance agents, real estate brokers, or financial services representatives. This manager's responsibilities differ markedly from those of the industrial sales manager and are largely shaped by the special nature of the "independent" representative's job. Typically, these sales representatives:

- Need a high degree of initiative and creativity to succeed

- Sell products or services that customers are not always convinced they need and that are not easily distinguishable from the many virtually identical products or services available in the marketplace

■ Acquire and service accounts that are at least as loyal to them as to the companies they represent

The manager must recruit and train new representatives to replace those who, inevitably, do not succeed. □

Because this type of sales position faces exceptional challenges, failure rates are high. But those who succeed realize substantial rewards. Generally, they are paid on a straight commission basis, a mathematical function of their productivity. This is certainly an appropriate approach in most cases because were the representative to join a competitor, most accounts would follow.

The unusual aspects of this type of sales position play a major role in determining both the manager's responsibilities and the type of bonus program that will encourage meeting those responsibilities most effectively. The manager must recruit and train new representatives to replace those who, inevitably, do not succeed. And, because the loss of a representative normally means a loss of accounts and a corresponding drop in the sales force's overall productivity, the manager must also ensure that high producers are not lured away by competitors.

It is also up to the manager to train and motivate existing representatives, particularly the lower producers, to increase their productivity. Because most companies compensate these representatives with straight commission and generally provide minimal reimbursement for out-of-pocket expenses, they probably make a profit even on the business of their low producers. But if the representatives themselves are not making an adequate income, they may be forced to seek other careers. Therefore, the manager must help these representatives improve their productivity and generate enough business to sustain themselves.

It is up to the manager to train and motivate existing representatives, particularly the lower producers, to increase their productivity. □

In light of these various responsibilities, the manager's performance is best evaluated by:

- Effectiveness in training existing representatives

- Ability to attract new producers who can provide the company with accounts that it would not otherwise have

- Skill in retaining productive sales representatives

These measures of sales management effectiveness are all reflected in the aggregate productivity of the manager's subordinates. And because their productivity is so closely linked to their level of income, their aggregate earnings are an appropri-

In some instances the "manager" has personal responsibility for accounts, in addition to supervisory responsibility. □

ate gauge of the manager's success in meeting those responsibilities. For this reason, a bonus based on a percentage of subordinates' aggregate earnings—the so-called "override" approach—is the most appropriate incentive compensation for this type of sales manager.

In some instances the "manager" has personal responsibility for accounts, in addition to supervisory responsibility. In such a situation, the reward system should follow the design principle appropriate for sales managers with respect to the results achieved by subordinates, and principles of sales rep compensation for personal production. A larger issue than compensation in the "producer-manager" scenario is the actual (or perceived) conflict in account assignment, which can undermine the mutual trust between manager and sales rep which is critical to sales force success.

Summary of General Approaches

In summary, the general approach to paying field sales managers follows a guideline indicating:

■ Override (percentage of subordinates' earnings) for manager of high-prominence sales force. *Example:* 10 percent of aggregate commissions (net of guarantee) paid to subordinates.

■ Bonus based on aggregate district or region goals for manager of industrial sales force. *Example:* 0 percent of salary for 90 percent of region volume goal or below, 20 percent of salary at 100 percent of goal, 40 percent of salary for 110 percent of goal and above; e.g., 2 percent of salary for earned per 1 percent of quota above threshold, to maximum of 110 percent of goal.

As long as the correct general approach is followed, any number of variations specific to the company's own situations can be incorporated in the program; for example, an override program might provide a higher percentage on the earnings of newer sales reps (and/or a declining percentage of commission), thus focusing the manager's earnings opportunity (and, presumably, attention) more closely on these reps who need help in maximizing productivity. Or an industrial sales manager's incentive could have a category of bonus which is product- or channel-specific, reflecting strategic needs.

Consequences of Incorrect Approach

Lastly, let's consider the conflicts created if the wrong approach is used. For example, if the override compensation method were used for the industrial manager, the *manager* would have a vested interest in assuring that the sales representatives' goals were as achievable as possible; on the surface, the concept of "the more the sales representatives earn the more the manager earns" should produce a harmonious working relationship. From the *company's* standpoint, however, sales goals must be linked to overall business goals and should, therefore, be achieved by requiring sales representatives to execute the specific account/product/market objectives set by the manager.

Through the results-oriented bonus, the manager has greater incentive to create this important link between the company's goals and representatives' goals. By establishing, rather than simply monitoring, the relevant, achievable objectives that will improve sales force productivity, the manager's own earnings can increase. This is a far stronger program than the override approach, which simply bases awards on the result itself and does not clearly delineate the intermediate milestones the sales force should meet in pursuing results.

Similarly, using a results-oriented bonus for the entrepreneur supervisor can also invite dysfunctional behavior. A bonus based on representatives' *average* productivity would not be appropriate; a manager might be inclined to weed out below-average producers to maximize the incentive award. From the company's standpoint, however, this would not be desirable because these underachievers are still individually profitable.

Using a results-oriented bonus for the entrepreneur supervisor can also invite dysfunctional behavior. □

This manager's focus needs to be on *aggregate* productivity; therefore, the override approach is ideal in motivating the manager to squeeze maximum productivity out of the high prominence sales force.

Chapter 11

Trends in Sales and the Future of Sales Compensation

By Bill O'Connell, Principal
and Lisa Bush Hankin, Senior Consultant
Sibson & Company

Introduction

Over the past few decades, the balance of power in the buying and selling equation has been shifting steadily toward the buyer. The reasons for this are many—better buyer information technology, consolidations wrought by mergers and acquisitions, the speed and volume of communication between buyers and sellers, fewer product advantages, constant pressure to deliver incremental profit, and so on. But when the discussion turns to how these changes will affect sales compensation, several trends stand out in stark relief. By far, the changing nature of companies' procurement processes and the enduring presence of the quality movement are and will continue to be the most profound influences on how salespeople must behave, sell, and be rewarded.

*At perhaps no
other time have
the individuals
involved in selling
been so
important to
their firms.* □

At perhaps no other time have the individuals involved in selling been so important to their firms. For instance, as a result of these changing procurement practices, companies are looking to their salespeople to behave more like businesspeople—that is, to manage the profitability of customer relationships and to make smart business-based decisions regarding whether and how to invest in a customer relationship. Companies are also working to retain a highly motivated sales force that will not only meet customer needs and develop customer relationships, but will also present a multiyear face to the customer.

As discrete transactions give way more and more to enduring buyer/seller relationships, sales compensation is becoming a tool with which to encourage sales force retention, to reward customer satisfaction, to encourage long-term buyer/seller relationships, and to acknowledge the importance of all the individuals involved in a customer relationship.

This chapter will provide some background on why these trends are so important to the future of sales compensation, as well as some insight into exactly what sales compensation may begin to look like in the years to come.

The New Approach to Procurement

The buy/sell event is undergoing a fundamental change as both buyers and sellers approach it with more initiative than ever before. On the one hand, buying companies face tremendous internal and competitive pressures to develop closer, more mutually beneficial supplier relationships to improve the true price/performance equation—the purchase and operating cost of the product or service relative to the increase in revenue or cost savings the company realizes because of its selections. Buyers' growing ability to measure ongoing operational costs, not just purchase pricing, has changed their procurement strategy from one of encouraging multiple suppliers to lower prices to a strategy of selecting and growing with one supplier.

Today's buyers—often a purchasing agent eligible for an incentive for evaluating, streamlining, and managing the company's supplier base—want to initiate the buy when *they* are ready, not when the seller wants to sell something. At the same time, purchasing agents' expectations have become more sophisticated and far-reaching. Whereas before they would

Today's buyers want to initiate the buy when they are ready, not when the seller wants to sell something. □

Today's customers are no longer merely buying a product; they are drawing on the resources of an entire organization to meet their specific needs. □

evaluate suppliers primarily on price and delivery measures, they now are also demanding more services from the selling organization, such as an easy buying process, new-product seminars, and tailored product catalogs, to name a few. Today's customers are no longer merely buying a product; they are drawing on the resources of an entire organization to meet their specific needs.

Owens & Minor, a Richmond-based distributor of hospital supplies, actually sells its ability to manage customers' inventory costs rather than lower purchase price for some of its major customers. By truly understanding its hospital customers' need to control inventory costs, this distributor has been able to expand its customer relationships in an environment where they could reasonably have been expected to contract. These expanded customer relationships have, however, required a significant investment in technology links for "real-time" inventory control and communication. In addition, the company now makes smaller, more frequent deliveries to its customers and works to save its customers money by systematically identifying wasteful supply use. At the same time, the Owens & Minor salesperson increasingly has to draw upon other members of the organization to create an account team that will truly be able to service customer needs and expand ongoing customer relationships.

The key point is this: The increasingly sophisticated demands of buyers are effectively "shaking out" the number of suppliers that are able *and* willing to meet these buyers' needs. (See Exhibit 11.1.) When today's buyers find suppliers that meet these criteria, they are more apt to consider solidifying a sole-source supplier relationship. Consequently, buyers are paying more attention to answering the question, "From whom should we *re*-buy?"

Establishing a stable and loyal customer base through ongoing relationships is at the heart of companies' survival. □

From the supplier's perspective, the stakes associated with this shift could not be higher. Establishing a stable and loyal customer base through ongoing relationships is at the heart of these companies' survival. Consider the results of a recent study of 200 of the Fortune 500 companies conducted by the University of Arizona. The study found that 35 percent of all goods and services purchased by manufacturers and 30 percent purchased by service firms are provided by single-source suppliers. At the same time, purchasing agents predict that they will be specifying the suppliers for more than 20 percent of their own

Exhibit 11.1   The Future of Buying and Selling

Buyers' increasingly sophisticated needs drive them toward sole-source and partnership arrangements with their suppliers.

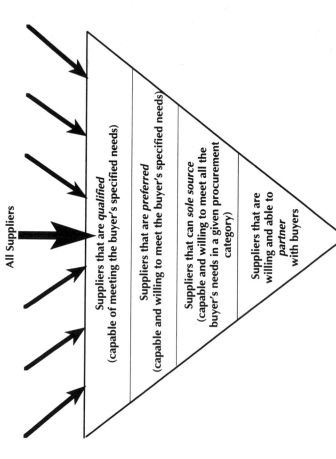

All Suppliers

Suppliers that are *qualified*
(capable of meeting the buyer's specified needs)

Suppliers that are *preferred*
(capable and willing to meet the buyer's specified needs)

Suppliers that can *sole source*
(capable and willing to meet all the
buyer's needs in a given procurement
category)

**Suppliers that are
willing and able to
partner
with buyers**

Source: Sibson & Company

supply base by the year 2000. Considering all this, it is not surprising that the researchers predict that the number of suppliers will decrease about 5 percent a year until the year 2000.

Those suppliers that can stay in the game stand to benefit by more than mere survival. A stable customer base will allow these companies to make sounder assessments of likely risks and rewards and, thereby, to increase their return on their investment decisions. Then, once suppliers understand and can operate with the new way customers buy, they must concentrate on living up to the "why" behind the buy—that is, meeting customers' quality expectations.

A major manifestation of the surge in quality consciousness is firms' increased expectations of their suppliers. □

The Continuing Quest for Quality

These changes in procurement practices are often a direct offshoot of companies' continuing quest for quality. Many companies—up to 40 percent or more, according to some studies—have embraced the quality movement to some degree. A major manifestation of this surge in quality consciousness is these firms' increased expectations of their suppliers. In other words, firms that have embraced quality principles expect their suppliers to meet or exceed that commitment while focusing on the end customer.

Moreover, buyers are not approaching these quality expectations in a vacuum. Access to more comprehensive information and technology has allowed buyers, for perhaps the first time, to truly gauge the effectiveness of products against the performance claims of the supplier. In fact, the sophistication of the buyer's data often surpasses that of the supplier. And its implications resonate throughout the selling organization. No longer is the onus solely on an individual salesperson to service a particular account. A customer's quality expectations now affect everyone in the organization who is involved with producing the product and servicing the account—from product development to billing to engineering to customer service to sales.

Clearly, both the how and the why behind a selling situation are changing and will continue to change. So the question is, how do sales and service support people need to sell and behave to be successful in this new environment? The answer to this

The sophistication of the buyer's data often surpasses that of the supplier. □

question lies, at least in part, in emerging sales compensation programs. These programs have a core objective in common: Reduce sales force turnover to keep a familiar face in front of the customer.

Keeping the Same Face in Front of the Customer

Suppliers that understand the realities of these new procurement practices and the importance of quality to their customers are more likely to be able to build the kind of stable and loyal customer base that is a critical success factor for companies today and in the future. The bottom line is, of course, that those suppliers that can establish these single-source relationships and make them profitable will survive and thrive. Beyond the survival question, a loyal and stable customer base can allow a company to make better investment decisions in areas such as new product development and to increase its return on those investments.

Suppliers that can establish single-source relationships and make them profitable will survive and thrive. □

To be sure, these changes are having a profound effect on sales forces in virtually every company as they struggle to stay

At no other time has the individual salesperson figured so prominently in maintaining and penetrating key customer accounts. ☐

abreast of the changing buyer/seller relationship. These changes in customer preferences and buying habits reinforce the need to present a consistent face to the customer. At no other time has the individual salesperson figured so prominently in maintaining and penetrating key customer accounts. As single-source supplier relationships grow in prominence, customers will be relying on the familiar and consistent presence not only of their salesperson, but also of the other key members of the account relationship team.

In this situation, sales compensation must do even more than measure, influence, and reward the appropriate behaviors of everyone involved in a customer relationship. It must also help retain those key selling team members.

One sales compensation trend that supports this need for companies to present a consistent "face" to customers is the increased use of teams and team selling rewards. Companies are also taking a longer-term view—that is, beyond one year—of sales compensation. To support these trends, sales compensation programs are more likely to:

■ Reward salespeople (and other key account team members) for follow-on buying by established customers, rather than just on the initial sale.

- Award bonuses for renewals of sales contracts—for example, in service companies—in subsequent years, even when another team member actually orchestrates the renewal.

- Provide recurring annual residuals for multiyear sales—for example, insurance policies.

- Award bonuses for achieving strategic objectives in the sales and relationship-building process, before the sale actually occurs.

- Recognize key account penetration and growth, as opposed to just growth in number of accounts.

All these sales compensation elements are designed to provide more incentive for the individual salesperson to stay with the company (and the newly established buyer/seller relationship) after the initial sale is complete.

Salesperson as Businessperson

A growing trend in sales management seeks to recast the salesperson in the role of a businessperson, who is responsible for making investment decisions and whose compensation is based on the *returns* from those investment decisions. In some cases, companies delegate the decisions of whether to make these investments to the salesperson—leaving it up to the salesperson to ensure that the capital outlay will result in increased sales—and pay the salesperson based, in part, on the ROI of his or her territory.

Companies may also give a salesperson a budget for the territory—leaving it up the individual to decide how to divide up that budget between such things as T&E, sales training, secretarial support, advertising and promotion, and so on, to achieve the highest return. One consumer products company provides its salespeople with an open understanding of sales support costs as well as a capped allowance to spend on the resources of their choice. Each salesperson must pay for any additional resources they request. Other companies, like one specialty chemical company, require salespeople to track expenses per customer so that they can develop an account-by-account P&L statement. As one sales executive put it, companies are "moving sales forces away from an emphasis on achieving gross margins to an emphasis on achieving a return on investment in each territory."

These plans treat the salesperson as a businessperson who is responsible for making decisions outside the traditional realm of sales—a development that mirrors the expanded roles of their buying counterparts in the procurement function.

A Prototype for the Future: Life-Cycle Sales Compensation

How will these trends manifest themselves in future sales compensation arrangements? As companies come to grips with these changes, they must recognize that sales compensation can be a powerful tool for retaining salespeople—something that becomes even more important as customers look for consistency in their sole-source providers. At the same time, companies are recognizing that the changes they need from their salespeople—a quality focus, the ability to deepen and strengthen customer relationships, the development of a business-focused mindset, among others—will take time. So to begin this development process, some companies have designed sales compensation programs that,

Retaining salespeople becomes even more important as customers look for consistency in their sole-source providers.□

With 100 percent commission plans, companies are lucky to retain 80 percent of their sales force a year. □

instead of paying 100 percent commission from day one, feature either a base salary and commissions plus a bonus opportunity, or commissions plus a bonus opportunity, depending on the company's overall business circumstances. After all, with 100 percent commission plans, companies are lucky to retain 80 percent of their sales force a year—an unacceptable retention rate in the emerging configuration of procurement practices.

Taking this concept a step further, some companies have embraced the concept of *life-cycle sales compensation* to address key turnover issues, as well as to increase productivity and efficiency. A life-cycle approach is designed to meet the needs of salespeople as they progress through all stages of their careers—from entry level through retirement. Companies developing such programs are operating under the assumption that salespeople will be less likely to look for opportunities to grow their earning potential elsewhere if their current employer provides ample opportunities that are tailored to their current needs throughout their careers. Not coincidentally, as people become more experienced, they also become more productive and profitable for the company, making retention even more imperative.

Here is how life-cycle compensation works. First, the company divides the salesperson's "life cycle" with the company into four specific time periods, based on an analysis of turnover, productivity, and business needs. For example, the first three years are the *intern* stage, followed by *experienced* in years 4 to 8, *seasoned* in years 9 to 24, and *retiree* in year 25 and beyond. (See Exhibit 11.2.) The actual number of and time for each stage will vary according to a company's needs and circumstances. Yet, any life-cycle compensation program should be fluid enough to evolve as the company's needs change.

Any life-cycle compensation program should be fluid enough to evolve as the company's needs change. □

Intern

During the first three years with the company, intern salespeople earn a base salary as they concentrate on learning about the business and the company's products and services. This base salary is highest during the training period and decreases gradually, to disappear completely at the end of the third year. In addition to this base salary, interns can earn commissions for sales. These commissions are shared with the intern's mentor; however, the commission rate for the intern increases annually, from 10 percent in the first year to 30 percent in

Exhibit 11.2   Life-Cycle Sales Compensation

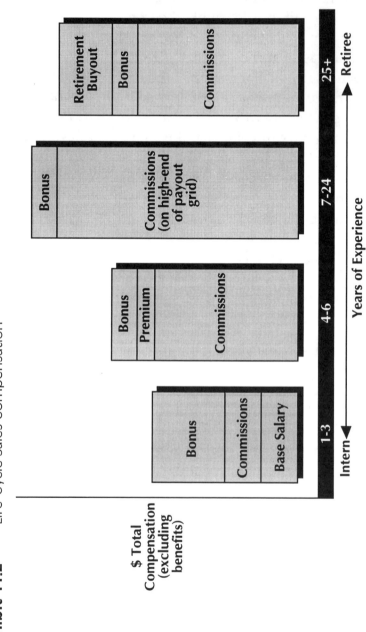

$ Total Compensation (excluding benefits)

| 1-3 | 4-6 | 7-24 | 25+ |

Intern ← → **Retiree**

Years of Experience

1-3:
- Bonus
- Commissions
- Base Salary

4-6:
- Bonus
- Premium
- Commissions

7-24:
- Bonus
- Commissions (on high-end of payout grid)

25+:
- Retirement Buyout
- Bonus
- Commissions

Source: Sibson & Company

the third year, while the commission rate for the mentor decreases annually, from 20 percent in the first year to 5 percent in the third year.

This intern plan is designed to allow the company to attract and retain a high caliber of entry-level salespeople. By paying these salespeople a base salary, the company can help these interns weather the ups and downs until they establish a firm foothold in the business. At the same time, it offers commissions and a bonus opportunity to encourage and reward higher productivity as the new salesperson begins to build a base of business. Concurrently, it rewards mentors for providing new employees with invaluable "on the job" training, which they might otherwise be reluctant to do, since it takes their focus off their own work.

Experienced

By the fourth year, the salesperson is considered experienced and the base salary component has been phased out completely. These experienced salespeople are now flying solo and growing business on their own. Total compensation is based largely on commissions, with a higher payout grid, a bonus opportunity based on annual productivity, and a premium paid for performance above a certain level. This stage lasts until the salesperson's sixth year with the company.

Seasoned

The salesperson's years 7 through 24 with the company are considered the seasoned period and are marked with their highest levels of productivity and profitability with the firm. This is also the period when the salesperson (and his or her established client base) are most attractive to talent-raiding competitors. Accordingly, this is when the company is the most vulnerable to turnover. These seasoned salespeople are growing their established customer relationships to become the customer's trusted advisor and to build quality books of business. Not surprisingly, these are the people a firm most needs to retain, and so it must provide these individuals with the highest earning potential in the plan. Commissions are on the high end of the payout grid and these seasoned salespeople are eligible for an annual productivity bonus, as well as an increased expense budget.

Retiree

Salespeople readying for retirement with more than 25 years with the company are

The salesperson's years 7 through 24 with the company are the period when the salesperson (and his or her established client base) are most attractive to talent-raiding competitors. □

eligible for commissions and a bonus, as well as a retirement buyout. During this period, the company and the retiree are working to transition the retiree's book of business and introduce these customers to experienced, but younger, salespeople. The retiree continues to provide counsel to the salespeople taking over these accounts for one year after retirement.

The company's retirement buyout is based on a combination of the retiree's age and length of service with the company. It is paid out over a three-year period as a percentage of customer assets he or she manages.

The company's retirement buyout is based on a combination of the retiree's age and length of service with the company. □

Into the Future

As these trends illustrate, both supplier companies and buyers have new and higher expectations of salespeople. Companies expect their salespeople to develop enduring preferred suppliers or single-source relationships, while also managing the profitability and ROI of those relationships. At the same time, buyers are approaching procurement more aggressively and with better information than ever before.

Buyers are approaching procurement more aggressively and with better information than ever before. □

These emerging dynamics will have far-reaching implications for sales compensation programs, as retention of an experienced and knowledgeable sales force becomes a key goal for most companies. Future sales compensation programs are likely to have several definable features—namely, team-based pay, more emphasis on pay for quality and customer satisfaction, a greater focus on long-term pay components, and more-sophisticated recognition programs.

In some companies, these sales compensation arrangements have already begun to take hold. But for those companies that have not aligned their sales compensation programs with this emerging reality, the future is fast approaching.

Chapter 12

The Case against Commissions

By William Keenan, Jr., Managing Editor
Sales & Marketing Management magazine

Introduction

There's a growing belief, arising out of the quality management movement, that efforts to link pay to performance—whether through commissions, bonuses, or incentives—will only undermine performance over the long run. Alfie Kohn, author of *Punished by Rewards* (Houghton Mifflin, 1993), and *No Contest: The Case Against Competition* (Houghton Mifflin, 1986, revised 1992), and who is probably the leading proponent of the case against commissions, went over the arguments for that case in a recent interview with *Sales & Marketing Management* magazine. The material that follows is based on that interview.

Kohn believes that incentives, bonuses, recognition awards, and other "bribes and goodies"—to use his own dismissive terms for these mainstays of many sales organizations—are nonproductive at best and counterproductive at worst.

> "What is not desired, and what ultimately feels punitive, is having the things we want used to control our behavior." ☐

Instead, he puts himself squarely in the center of the quality movement, arguing in favor of such things as employee involvement, continuous improvement, participative management, customer satisfaction, and other shibboleths of the modern manager. In fact, says Kohn, "When I'm asked to summarize *Punished by Rewards* in a sentence, I say, 'You can only get quality by working with people, never by doing things *to* people.' And the second sentence, when I am permitted one, raises hackles: 'Rewards, like punishments, are ways of doing things *to* people.'" To elaborate, he adds, "The manager who talks about continuous improvement, or customer satisfaction, or collaboration in the workplace is being inconsistent by clinging to what is effectively a manipulative strategy of dangling goodies in front of people to get them to perform. The rewards themselves—a trip to Hawaii, a stereo system, an extra five grand—are highly desired. But what is not desired, and what ultimately feels punitive, is having the things we want used to control our behavior."

What's Wrong with Rewards?

"If the question is, 'Do rewards motivate people?'" Kohn says, "the answer is, 'Yes, absolutely, they motivate people to get rewards.' But that's usually at the expense of excellence at what they're doing over the long haul." Rewards, whether they come in the form of commissions, bonuses, incentives, or recognition, says Kohn, are good for only one thing—assuring temporary compliance.

That's evident, at least in part, in many sales managers' preoccupation with issues of compensation and rewards. "No matter how many times we jigger the compensation schemes or come up with new cutesy contests and reward tactics, they continue to have a short half-life," says Kohn. "People aren't pleased with them, but they never realize that the problem is with the very idea of intrinsic motivators themselves. Fiddling around with the details of implementation won't give us a system that works. The problem is with the completely inadequate theory of human motivation on which the very idea of sales commissions and other rewards rests."

Managers continue to use such programs, Kohn argues, because that's what they know. It's the way they were managed and taught and raised as children: Do this, and you'll get that. And the limited, short-term results of such reward systems blind most

"The problem is with the completely inadequate theory of human motivation on which the very idea of sales commissions and other rewards rests." □

managers to the long-term negative effects on performance.

"Rewards are basically ways of controlling people—of doing things *to* people," Kohn says. "That's why I say that rewards and punishments are not opposites at all, but two sides of the same coin."

> *"Rewards and punishments are not opposites at all, but two sides of the same coin."* ☐

Finally, says Kohn, rewards are easy. "It takes no talent, no time, and no skill to say, 'Here is what I'll give you if you jump through my hoops.'"

Salespeople, on the other hand, are preoccupied with their compensation plans and raise such a hue and cry when changes in compensation are announced because they've become dependent on compensation as an extrinsic motivator. "If you have destroyed people's love of work by getting them dependent on money," says Kohn, "then you would expect them to become more interested in money. If you deprive people of a sense of control over their own work lives, so that they feel manipulated, then all you leave them to focus on is how many bucks this is worth."

When there is talk of a change in the compensation plan, says Kohn, "many salespeople and other employees will feel—reasonably enough—that this is going to be an attempt to screw them, and I don't blame them for being worried, given the track record of lots of executives."

Survey research since the 1940s shows that when you ask people what matters most to you about a job, compensation ranks fifth or sixth on the list after such factors as interesting work, variety of tasks, collegiality, and others. "Despite being battered with intrinsic motivators, despite being controlled with commissions and other manipulative tactics," says Kohn, "people ultimately care most about things other than compensation."

"People ultimately care most about things other than compensation." □

The Effects of Competition

All reward systems are bad, says Kohn, but the worst are those that involve some form of competition. So an incentive program that promises a trip to Tahiti for the top five producers or the top 10 percent of your salespeople does infinitely more harm than the program that offers the same trip to anyone who tops his or her last year's sales performance by 10 percent. The difference is that the latter program gives everyone—at least in theory—an equal chance, but the former creates an artificial scarcity in which one salesperson's chance of getting the reward is reduced by the next salesperson's chance of getting it.

Competition raises the anxiety level of salespeople, putting them under greater stress. ☐

Competition for rewards will have several predictable effects. For one, coordination and effective exchange of talents and resources will be impeded if not eliminated. "It is irrational for one salesperson to share what he knows if someone else's success will come at his expense due to a competitive structure in rewards," says Kohn. Another effect is that competition raises the anxiety level of salespeople, putting them under greater stress. "If I'm worried that you are going to snatch that trip to Hawaii and step on my face because that's what the system demands," says Kohn, "I'm not going to be able to attend to my work in the most efficient way possible."

The predictability of competition in many cases can also be a negative factor, says Kohn. "If you tell me that the reason I should work hard is to win a prize, I may decide quite quickly that Jeanine or George down the hall is more likely to win than I, so why should I bother?"

"There is also research showing that when people compete, they are more likely to explain the results of that competition in terms of factors beyond their control—factors like luck or market forces, or the size of their territory. Whereas in a noncompetitive environment people are more likely to explain their results in terms of effort—clearly the more useful way to think when it comes to helping people to do a better job the next time."

Pit salespeople one against the other, says Kohn, and what you can expect is a decline in performance over the long term, and erosion of self-esteem ("since I come to think of myself as competent only in terms of how many people I have beaten"), and a less friendly, collaborative, supportive environment. "The central message that all competition teaches is that everyone else is a potential obstacle to my success. That will not only have a detrimental effect on performance, but will also significantly undermine the quality of life where I work every day."

Pit salespeople one against the other, and what you can expect is a decline in performance over the long term. □

A Pay-for-Performance Primer

Turnover and plateauing—two problems common to virtually every sales organization and that very few managers have been successful in dealing with, are precisely

The use of rewards undermines people's creativity. □

the sort of symptom that one would expect, based on the research on the use of sales commissions and other strategies that rely on "carrots and sticks," says Kohn. "More than 70 studies have shown that when people are led to think about how much money they are going to make as a result of what they are doing every day, they will come to lose interest in whatever they had to do to get the money. The task comes to be seen as less interesting in its own right."

Research also shows that the use of rewards undermines people's creativity, says Kohn, "by getting people to think in terms of snagging the goodie as expeditiously as possible." He uses the analogy of a rat in a maze, where "the point is to rush toward the cheese in the way that has proved most effective in the past, with as little time as possible spent on incidental issues that might not help me today." In other words, the more people are reward-driven, the less likely they are to take risks or play hunches that might not pay off. And when you take away rewards, Kohn says, "research shows that people are more likely to spontaneously choose more difficult tasks. That's because, when we're not told to think about money, we humans like to challenge ourselves to reach beyond what we are able to do now, to acquire new skills, and to wrestle with new ideas."

Extrinsic motivators undermine intrinsic motivators, the research seems to be saying; you can't have both. Intrinsic motivation—which means that you love what you do—and extrinsic motivation—artificial inducements like money, trophies, trips, grades, and the like—are generally not additive. You don't get more motivation when you put the two together. In fact, Kohn is arguing that you get less—the extrinsic form eats away at the intrinsic motivation. As Kohn puts it: "If you tell me that the reason I have to sell more product is that I'm going to take home more money, then the likely effect is that I will come to see the selling itself as a tedious prerequisite to getting the goodie. Then, in the next go-round, I'm going to have absolutely no reason to get involved in what I'm doing other than to make more money. That's a recipe for burnout, stress, and dissatisfaction with my current job."

The more you control people with money, the more their intrinsic motivation evaporates. □

The more you control people with money, Kohn says, the more their intrinsic motivation evaporates, and the more you have to continue to control people with money. It's a self-fulfilling prophecy. That's why the typical sales manager will say, "You see,

"We have reinforced ourselves into a box from which it's hard to escape." □

unless I tell them this is what you'll get for bringing the numbers up, salespeople won't do it." Kohn responds: "That's not a reflection of some fact about human nature, it's a reflection of what their reward systems have done in the past."

Managers continue to use reward systems, says Kohn, because that's what they know. It's the way they were managed, and taught, and raised as children. "Do this and you'll get that"—it's the very linchpin of American society. And that's why few managers can see beyond tinkering with the rewards, the prizes, or the formulas. "We have reinforced ourselves into a box from which it's hard to escape," says Kohn, "so now we just compare one system to another instead of questioning the very premise."

The real alternative to manipulating people with commissions and prizes, says Kohn, is not a bigger, better incentive plan, or a more intricate payout formula for commissions or bonuses. "Choosing extrinsic motivator A versus extrinsic motivator B doesn't get anywhere near the heart of the problem. The very idea of using artificial inducements to control people's performance is what is at issue here. The real alternative is to move toward democracy, to move toward working with people and giving them fundamental choices about how their jobs are done."

Beyond Rewards

If not rewards, then what? What's the democratic, collaborative alternative to manipulation by rewards? How *should* salespeople be paid? It's in answer to questions like that that Kohn's argument is most vulnerable. Not because he doesn't have an answer, but because his answer throws the question back upon those asking the questions. "When I speak to executives and they ask, 'How do I pay people?' I say pay them well, pay them fairly, and then do everything in your power to take their minds off money because the more you get people to come to work in the morning thinking about how much more they are going to get depending on what they do, the more you undermine the quality of work and interest in work over the long term."

And what's fair in Kohn's view? "That's something that employees have to come together to decide over a period of time. It does make sense to me that someone who

The real alternative is to move toward democracy. □

Even good ideas can't be shoved down people's throats. □

has a larger territory, and therefore has to put in more hours, would be paid more. But there are any number of criteria that could be used. You could pay everyone equally, or you could pay on the basis of need. You could pay on the basis of experience or seniority or on the basis of market factors. I'm not strongly arguing for one system over another.

"The decisions about what constitutes fairness," Kohn says, "have to come out of a collaborative conversation—it's not something to be decided by top executives alone."

In fact, says Kohn, you won't solve your problems simply by abolishing commissions. "If you walk into a meeting of your sales force on Monday and announce that you're going to straight salary and off commissions effective immediately, salespeople are not going to leap out of their seats and say, 'Hooray! Now we can be intrinsically motivated.' Even good ideas can't be shoved down people's throats."

Moving away from what Kohn calls "carrot and stick" psychology is a necessary step, but that step alone won't guarantee an improvement in the health of an organization or the quality of performance. "You might argue the other way around," says

Kohn, "that only when you have the ingredients of quality in place can you begin to eliminate reward systems. If people feel their jobs are pointless, if they feel that everyone else is an obstacle to their own success, if they feel controlled and powerless and there is no collaboration going on, then you are not going to get away with eliminating the only inducement they have left to do anything—which is money."

Instead—and companies moving along the quality improvement road might have an advantage here—managers first have to create a safe environment, an environment "where people understand they are not going to be penalized or humiliated for speaking their minds," says Kohn. And once that environment is in place, he adds, companies can begin the "long-term, difficult process of discussion about what is happening in the organization, asking people about how they experience their jobs, and each other, and the boss, and their paychecks. Then setting aside time for a program of discussion and education, of having people read things on this issue and discuss them, or attend seminars. And slowly, over a period of time, making changes that feel rooted in people's changing sensibilities about work."

Kohn's message is not, strictly speaking, to abolish reward systems. □

The correct question is not, "What's the alternative to rewards?" The correct question, according to Kohn, is "If rewards are undermining interest and excellence, how do we get interest and excellence?" And, says Kohn, "That's an importantly different question from 'Hey, I've got something that works now. What are you going to give me instead if I drop it?'"

Ultimately, Kohn's message is not, strictly speaking, to abolish reward systems. Instead, it's to "listen more and talk less, work *with* and don't do *to,* and with problems large and small, ask employees what they think you can do to solve this problem." What he thinks you'll eventually hear is that you should abolish reward systems.

A Glossary of Sales Compensation Terms

The listing below is not meant to be comprehensive, but includes all of the major compensation-related terms used in this book.

Account relationship compensation—Pay that is contingent upon account management, account penetration, or customer satisfaction.

Account retention incentives—A reward for maintaining a specific account at a certain minimum sales volume throughout the year, or for maintaining total sales volume for existing accounts at a certain level.

Barriers to entry—Minimum educational or experience qualifications required for an entry-level sales postition which may have an impact on compensation levels, particularly on the level of base or guaranteed compensation.

Base salary—A guarateed minimum compensation level, paid at regular intervals, regardless of performance levels.

Bonus—An opportunity to earn an additional pre-established level of compensation by meeting a goal or a series of goals. These goals can be related to sales volume, customer satisfaction, new product sales, new accounts, etc.

Channel management incentives—Incentives paid to a manufacturer's employee who holds full or partial responsibility for sales through a partucular distribution channel.

Combination plans—Any sales compensation plan that includes both salary and pay-at-risk, whether in the form of commissions or bonuses. Combination plans can be low-risk (where total compensation levels are more or less predictable) or high risk (where there is a higher degree of uncertainty about total pay levels).

Commission—The sales rep's predetermined share of a business outcome (whether of a single transaction or an annual sales volume).

Commission accelerators—An extra commission (or enhanced commission rate) for sales that exceed a pre-established volume (or other) threshold.

Commission pool—When commissions are paid into a pool, rather than to an individual, usually applying to non-sales contributors to a team selling arrangement and paid out according to a weighted formula determined by an individual's "contribution to the sale."

Customer satisfaction bonus—A bonus that is contingent upon customer satisfaction levels, usually measured by a formal customer satisfaction survey.

Disguised salary—Any combination of salary and commission which results in a predictable, stable income stream.

Distributor incentive—A commission or discount allowed to distributors or manufacturers' reps which is contingent upon sales volume or other objective sales goals.

Double crediting—Arrangements under which two individuals recieve the full commission for the same sale.

Draw against commission—An advance against future commission earnings; usually to flatten out income fluctuations.

Expense reimbursement—Reimbursement for out-of-pocket expenses, particularly mileage and hotel costs, to assure that a whole territory is covered.

First dollar plan—Salespeople begin to earn commission on their first sales. There are no performance thresholds salespeople must reach before beginning to earn commissions.

"First-year revenues" commission—A commission that takes into account all revenues accruing during the first year of business with a new customer, regardless of whether the salesperson continues to call on that account. Usually used to facilitate the transfer of customers from sales to account management.

Interim pay plan—A temporary pay plan or compensation bridge, usually including some element of guarateed pay, offered to assist new salespeople through an initial learning curve.

Leverage—The percentage of a salesperson's total pay which is "at risk," or subject to pay-for-performance contingencies.

Life-cycle sales compensation—A sales compnesation plan that changes, both in terms of payment vehicles, and of the percentage of pay-at-risk, over the course of a salesperson's career, from trainee to retiree.

Milestone-based incentives—An interim pay plan for new salespeople that is tied to training and development objectives rather than sales performance goals.

Multiplier—A commission enhancer that applies when certain goals (e.g., customer satisfaction) are met.

"Net new business" incentive—A payment based on the difference between the amount of new business a salesperson brings in and the amount of existing business that's been lost.

Non-recoverable draw—When draw payments exceed earned commissions and the salesperson keeps the difference.

Override commission—A commission paid on someone else's commission—usually as a way of compensating sales managers.

Pay-at-risk—The percentage of the total sales compensation plan that is directly contingent upon productivity or performance factors.

Performance premium—The percentage difference in total compensation between an average performer and a top sales performer under the same pay plan.

Progressive commissions—Commission rates that increase as sales volume exceeds successively higher thresholds.

Recognition programs—Any program that offers public congratulations/recognition for attainment of certain performance levels (Salesman of the Year, Million

Dollar Club, e.g.) in lieu of or in addition to cash rewards.

Recoverable draw—If draw payments exceed earned commissions and the salesperson is obliged to pay back the difference.

Regressive commissions—Commission rates that decrease as sales volume passes successively higher thresholds. Rule of ten—no single measure contributing to incentive compensation should account for less than ten percent of total compensation. The assumption is that a factor accounting for less than ten percent will fail to change the behavior of the salesperson.

Sales contests—Short-term incentive programs which are separate from the regular sales compensation plan, and which may involve merchandise or travel awards as well as cash.

Sales rep prominence—The degree of influence that an indvidual sales rep has on sales volume.

Secure compensation—Base salary or guaranteed compensation, not tied to sales volume or other performance factors.

"Soft landing" bonus plans—Bonus plans in which a significant portion of the total bonus is paid out even if the salesperson falls short of quota.

Split commissions—When the established commission for a sale is divided among two or more individuals, sometimes used in team selling situations, or in field training situations where a veteran sales rep is accompanying a novice salesperson.

Straight commission—A sales compensation plan that is comprised only of commissions; there is no base salary component of the plan.

"Stretch" goals or bonus—An additional payout, or incremental commission, paid on attaining goals that exceed a salesperson's expected performance levels.

Temporary guarantee—A guaranteed minimum salary for a limited period of time; usually offered to new sales reps to give them time to reach full productivity.

Threshold—A sales revenue level that must be reached before commission or bonus payments are made; usually expressed as a percentage of projected business.

Transactional incentives—Pay, like most commissions, that is contingent upon each individual sale to a customer.

Transition pay plan—A short-term pay plan that may be put into place during the implementation of a new sales compensation plan. It may be a plan which offers to pay salespeople under either the old or the new plan, whichever is higher, or pay a guaranteed percentage of the old plan, for a specified period of time.

Index